"Insightful, practical, stimulating, p̲[...] lenge our own cultural assumptions and help sharpen our skills in the art and science of teaching anything to anyone, anywhere."

Américo Saavedra, leadership development consultant and teacher/facilitator, Reach Beyond

"Jim Plueddemann's book *Teaching Across Cultures* is a road trip. After each bend in the road, teacher and travelers reflect on discoveries never seen before though looked at many times."

Mark H. Senter III, professor emeritus of educational ministry, Trinity Evangelical Divinity School

"When teaching across cultures, even experienced teachers need a paradigm shift. Jim Plueddemann's teaching model perceives the learner as a purposeful traveler. Plueddemann's lively stories weave throughout the book. I recommend it to missionaries, teachers, pastors, and seminarians—really everyone who wishes to interact with others in this global village."

Judy Tao, missionary trainer and professor, Taiwan

"Jim's breakthrough thinking combining theory and practice in a truly transformative learning cycle is both profound and simple at the same time. It is profound enough to guide anyone who desires to teach in any culture yet simple enough to remember and apply time after time. We often read books which are complex but ultimately superficial. Reading *Teaching Across Cultures* is refreshingly simple but startlingly profound. Disciple makers, preachers, and teachers anywhere will profit by a thorough study and practice of this book."

Charles A. Davis, former director of TEAM, author of *Making Disciples Across Cultures*

"In this exceptionally clear and engaging book the reader is introduced to the challenges of teaching across cultures through both story and theory. The book wins the reader by Plueddemann's willingness to tell stories about his own struggles to teach well crossculturally. The author skillfully challenges readers to think through their assumptions about what good education is and gently points out how our pedagogical preferences might affect our ability to teach effectively across cultures. Highly recommended for anyone who wants to grow as a teacher."

James Wilhoit, professor of core studies and Scripture Press professor of Christian education, Wheaton College

"This book is a gift to the global church. Filled with wisdom and experience gleaned across cultures and over time, it offers valuable principles and practical examples to make teaching what it should be—life changing. If you're teaching or training in another culture, make sure you pack this book."

Frank Newell, professor, Alexandria School of Theology, Egypt

"Dr. James E. Plueddemann, veteran missionary, teacher, and professor, has effectively debunked the myth that teachers merely transfer knowledge to their students. Through the use of numerous metaphors, diagrams, stories, and personal life experiences, he has demonstrated that successful teachers must combine knowledge with an understanding of the culture and experience of students. This extremely rich and practical book should be required reading for all crosscultural missionaries and teachers."

Samuel Waje Kunhiyop, author of African Christian Ethics, professor and former general secretary of ECWA, Nigeria

"The depth and breadth of Plueddemann's experience and relationships is inspiring and instructive. The fact that it covers so many different contexts is a reflection of the deep commitment and faithfulness that, in turn, produced this helpful resource. Jim is not a mere teacher but instead is a humble, life-long learner, leader, and trainer. He brings the theory down to the ground—in context—in community. Added to that, at the end of each chapter there are voices from all over the globe. And Jim knows that he doesn't know everything . . . or much sometimes! But that is the power of his approach and this tool. This is a tool for trainers and learners. It was a joy to walk through this book, seeing his heart and the depth of his commitment to the subject over the long haul."

Greg H. Parsons, Frontier Ventures, Pasadena, California

TEACHING

ACROSS

CULTURES

CONTEXTUALIZING EDUCATION
FOR GLOBAL MISSION

James E. Plueddemann

IVP Academic

An imprint of InterVarsity Press
Downers Grove, Illinois

InterVarsity Press
P.O. Box 1400, Downers Grove, IL 60515-1426
ivpress.com
email@ivpress.com

InterVarsity Press® is the book-publishing division of InterVarsity Christian Fellowship/USA®, a movement of students and faculty active on campus at hundreds of universities, colleges, and schools of nursing in the United States of America, and a member movement of the International Fellowship of Evangelical Students. For information about local and regional activities, visit intervarsity.org.

All Scripture quotations, unless otherwise indicated, are taken from The Holy Bible, New International Version®, NIV®. Copyright © 1973, 1978, 1984, 2011 by Biblica, Inc.™ Used by permission of Zondervan. All rights reserved worldwide. www.zondervan.com. The "NIV" and "New International Version" are trademarks registered in the United States Patent and Trademark Office by Biblica, Inc.™

While any stories in this book are true, some names and identifying information may have been changed to protect the privacy of individuals.

"When Humility Backfired" on page 67 is taken from Cross-Cultural Connections *by Duane Elmer. Copyright ©2009 by Duane Elmer. Used by permission of InterVarsity Press, P.O. Box 1400, Downers Grove, IL 60515, USA. www.ivpress.com.*

Cover design: Cindy Kiple
Interior design: Daniel van Loon
Images: chalkboard illustration: © Sonya_illustration / iStockphoto
*   world map illustration: © NatanaelGinting / iStockphoto*
Author photo: ©2018 William Koechling

ISBN 978-0-8308-5221-5 (print)
ISBN 978-0-8308-7372-2 (digital)

Library of Congress Cataloging-in-Publication Data

Names: Plueddemann, Jim, author.
Title: Teaching across cultures : contextualizing education for global
* mission / James E. Plueddemann, IVP Academic.*
Description: Downers Grove, IL : InterVarsity Press, [2018] | Includes
* bibliographical references.*
Identifiers: LCCN 2018028339 (print) | LCCN 2018034436 (ebook) | ISBN
* 9780830873722 (eBook) | ISBN 9780830852215 (print : alk. paper) | ISBN*
* 9780830873722 (digital)*
Subjects: LCSH: Missions—Study and teaching. | Christian education. |
* Christianity and culture.*
Classification: LCC BV2090 (ebook) | LCC BV2090 .P58 2018 (print) | DDC
* 268--dc23*
LC record available at https://lccn.loc.gov/2018028339

P   25   24   23   22   21   20   19   18   17   16   15   14   13   12   11   10   9   8   7   6   5   4   3   2   1

Y   37   36   35   34   33   32   31   30   29   28   27   26   25   24   23   22   21   20   19   18

Dedicated with gratitude to professors and mentors
now with the Lord who so patiently encouraged this contrarian learner

Dr. Mary LeBar
Wheaton College

Dr. Lois LeBar
Wheaton Graduate School

Dr. Ted Ward
Michigan State University

as well as leaders in the ECWA Christian Education Department, Nigeria

Rev. David Buremoh
who first had the vision for Christian Education in ECWA

Rev. Samuila Kure
who took over from me making the department ever more effective

Rev. Philip Gambo
powerful teacher and motivator in Christian Education

CONTENTS

FOREWORD

Duane H. Elmer

FEW PEOPLE IN THIS WORLD have done more traveling, more reading, more reflection, and more careful analysis on culture, education, and the mission of God than Dr. James Plueddemann. In this book he turns his attention to the topic of teaching and culture. In doing so, he challenges the dangerously common assumption that we can teach elsewhere just like we teach in our home culture.

This summary alone should inspire careful attention if not serious dialogue around this book. Jim's credentials include thirteen years partnering with Nigerian church leaders to build a national Christian education program for the exploding Christian population and to effectively teach the Scriptures. Different cultural values and traditions needed to be understood before launching any program that would be successful. Understanding grew as he studied the home, school, business world, health professions, NGOs, and other nonformal learning situations. Through observing, questioning, listening, and dialogue, insights emerged that became integral in the educational activities of the local church.

As the international director of SIM (Serving in Mission) for ten years, Jim taught in scores of countries with disciplined attention to how people in other cultures learn, grow, and change. Now, in retirement, his many teaching invitations are potent witness to how well received he is and how people want further exposure to his ideas. His lifetime of gathered insights are now available to us as a gift in the form of this book. The reader will be enriched by (1) principles of teaching in another culture, (2) stories of successes and failures from dozens of countries, (3) purposeful attention to the cultural context, and (4) taking the posture of a learner before entering the teacher role.

Most books of this nature tend toward applied how-to books, or they tend toward theoretical "What does the research say?" books. One genius of *Teaching Across Cultures* is the masterful weaving of both theory and practice. The weave is even more apparent if one reads the footnotes that often supply the theoretical background for a particular principle. But another genius element in the tapestry of this book is the use of Scripture, important to those of us who believe there is truth that guides us. So here you have a wonderful trilogy of good theory and good practice within a biblical framework.

It should be noted that *Teaching Across Cultures* will be helpful to virtually every audience whether the differences are cultural, generational, ethnic, gender, or regional. We all want to be better teachers. We are all concerned with outcomes as a result of our teaching; this book takes us there as well. Teaching Scripture is always intended to promote obedience to Christ, our Lord. This book helps us achieve that most important goal.

ACKNOWLEDGMENTS

I've been working on this book all my life. My first teachers were my parents, Edwin and Mary Margret Kirkpatrick Plueddemann. My mother was a trained teacher who consistently integrated principles of learning with parenting, whether it was modeling joyful creativity or setting rules for trombone practice. I learned from my dad as he interacted in intense theological discussions in our living room and at church. His joy of living was evident as he played with neighborhood children at the park, tinkered with his chemistry set at work, or preached his heart out in a rural church.

Most of all I am grateful beyond words for my wife, Carol Savage Plueddemann. I could not have written this book without her kind, persistent encouragement and her skillful editing. Her crosscultural experiences growing up in Ecuador, serving for thirteen years together in Nigeria, traveling with me to over sixty countries, and then serving as minister of congregational life in our church in Illinois equip her in a unique way as my valued adviser for this book.

Others have been kind and helpful in reading early drafts of the book and making valuable recommendations, including Harold Myra, Charlie Davis, Duane Elmer, Shari Plueddemann, and Tabitha Plueddemann. Thanks also to Lisa Anderson Umaña for soliciting examples of teaching across cultures from the Latin American perspective.

Many thanks to Rob Ribbe and HoneyRock Camp, the "Northwoods campus" of Wheaton College, for providing an idyllic place for concentrated writing.

INTRODUCTION

Go and make disciples of all nations . . . teaching them to obey
everything I have commanded you.

MATTHEW 28:19-20

Education without values, as useful as it is, seems
rather to make man a more clever devil.

C. S. LEWIS

I ONCE CHAUFFEURED an American professor around Nigeria. This man was one of the most sought-after teachers in the United States, yet his teaching was almost incomprehensible to rural Nigerian audiences. I stepped in to interpret his American slang into Nigerian English. He began, "Now what I'm going to tell you will rot your socks!" I translated to an audience wearing sandals, "Pay attention! What this man is about to tell you is very important." Then, "This lesson will shoot you out of the saddle!" I assured our shocked listeners, "Don't worry—he wants you to pay close attention to an important point. He doesn't want to shoot you."

TEACHERS FROM EVERYWHERE TO EVERYWHERE

We live in a dizzyingly connected world where teachers come from everywhere and go everywhere. The trend is both exhilarating and bewildering. Guatemalans teach in India, Koreans in Zambia, Americans in China, Canadians in Cuba, Indians in South Sudan, and Nigerians in the United States. Their qualifications for teaching are usually academic credentials from their home country based on the mastery of subject matter, often overlooking the importance of understanding the host culture. The desire to teach around the world is heartening, but the potential dangers of irrelevance, misunderstandings, wasted resources, and other unintended consequences are real.

Effective crosscultural teachers possess three competencies: (1) they've mastered the *content* to be taught, (2) they appreciate the *cultural values*, needs, and context of the host learners, and (3) they foster *connections* between the content and the context of the learners. Without these three competencies many crosscultural teachers have limited effectiveness.

Teachers often seem to assume that knowledge alone will in some mysterious way lead to better living. In Scripture, the examples of Israel and the early church suggest that knowledge is necessary but far from sufficient for godly living.

I taught a course at Trinity Evangelical Divinity School called "Teaching the Bible in Intercultural Settings." At the end of the course one student observed, "This course isn't just about teaching the Bible and it isn't just about other cultures; it's about how to teach anything to anybody, anywhere." If we understand only our own culture, we can teach some things to some people. When we learn to teach effectively across cultures, we can teach almost anything to anybody, anywhere.

THEOLOGICAL ASSUMPTIONS

What is Christian education? Is it Sunday school? Christian primary or secondary schools? Christian colleges? My belief is that Christian education is all of these and much more. Teaching that is pleasing to God builds on all of God's truth and fosters the development of learners into all God intended them to become. Much of so-called Christian education does not meet this standard. There are three potential pitfalls for teachers: ignoring God's truth, disregarding the development of the learner, and not connecting truth with life.

Philosopher Arthur Holmes popularized the concept that "all truth is God's truth wherever it is found."[1] He argued that there is no

---

[1]Arthur F. Holmes, *All Truth Is God's Truth* (Downers Grove, IL: InterVarsity Press, 1979), 8. Holmes makes the case that the Bible and early church writers emphasized the importance of the study of God's *world* as well as God's *Word*. Since God created everything that exists, everything humans study is a study of the sacred.

difference between true secular and sacred knowledge.[2] Of course our understanding of God's truth in this life will never be complete, so we must cultivate a deep sense of humility along with curiosity. The other danger is that we are not always capable of distinguishing between truth and falsehood, which again requires humility and honest investigation. God's truth is found in his Word and in his world. All of the academic disciplines, then, can take nourishment from God's truth.

Bodies of knowledge, whether rules for playing soccer, advanced trigonometry, skills in brewing coffee, or themes in the Pentateuch, are not ends in themselves but have the potential for promoting the development of persons into all God intended.

Human development is multifaceted. We are reminded that "Jesus grew in wisdom and in stature and in favor with God and all the people" (Lk 2:52 NLT). Similarly, Samuel, living in a dark era of Israel's history, "continued to grow in stature and in favor with the LORD and with people" (1 Sam 2:26). Holistic human development is mental, physical, spiritual, and social. The intended outcome then of teaching in any culture is to build on important bodies of knowledge in the pursuit of integrated human development.

Practically any teaching method has the potential of promoting human development. Lectures, sermons, demonstrations, group discussions, online courses, mentoring, and many more methods might be used to grow and develop the learner. Of course, all these pedagogies also have the potential of ignoring God's truth and disregarding the development of the student. The key for effective teaching is forging that never-before-seen connection between content and the life of the learner.

I'm convinced that this overarching principle of communicating information in a way that promotes human development is universally

---

[2]I hesitate to use the term *knowledge*. When I'm talking about cognitive content, I use the term *bodies of knowledge*. I'm aware that individuals possess *practical knowledge* as well as *theoretical knowledge*. See Michael Polanyi, *The Tacit Dimension* (Garden City, NY: Anchor Books, 1966). Polanyi discusses the importance of personal knowledge or tacit knowledge as harmonious with scientific knowledge. His insightful observation is "we can know more than we can tell" (p. 4). The Hebrew word *yāḏaʿ* is translated "to know," but it is also used as a term for making love. Adam "knew" Eve and they had a son (Gen 4:1). The Hebrew concept of knowing is much more than the cognitive.

effective. With crosscultural adaptations, it is the key to teaching effectively in every situation anywhere.

Many humanistic educators hold values in common with Christian educators: that individuals possess dignity, that cultivating human development is a worthy endeavor, that individuals thrive only in community, and that loving one's neighbor is an admirable rule of life. I hope this book will be helpful to those who don't claim to be Christian, as well as those who embrace a Christian worldview.

I trust the book will be beneficial for teaching in *informal* settings such as parenting and in *formal* school settings. I hope it will be useful for *nonformal* educators such as youth pastors, camp counselors, home Bible study leaders, and also for those in missions and development organizations around the world teaching literacy, health, business, or agriculture.

CULTURAL ASSUMPTIONS

The focus of the book is how to teach people who are different from oneself. In a sense all human beings are unique, so all education is crosscultural. My wife declares that every marriage is crosscultural even if husband and wife have the same racial and cultural background.

Age differences magnify cultural differences. I teach a high school Sunday school class in our church. Understanding the world of a fifteen-year-old girl or a seventeen-year-old boy is a crosscultural challenge for this older professor who taught for thirteen years in Africa and in graduate schools for twenty-five years. Whether I teach a doctoral seminar in South Korea, a workshop in Panama, a masters-level class in Ethiopia, or a children's Sunday school class in Nigeria, I face unexpected cultural challenges about teaching and learning. The only way to teach effectively in all these settings is to seek an understanding of the learners' culture. So I cautiously propose that this book is about *how to teach almost anything to anyone, anywhere.*

EDUCATIONAL IMPLICATIONS

Theological assumptions have profound educational implications. I write from the viewpoint of a Christian, seeking to align my educational philosophy with Scripture. Readers who do not hold these assumptions will still find this book useful since many of the educational principles in it are commonly accepted by the broader educational community.

I'm a developmentalist.[3] This means that the central aim of education is to foster the lifelong holistic development of the individual in community. My desire in teaching is that individuals will develop into all God intended them to become.

The following list describes educational implications that flow from my theological assumptions. Each of these assumptions carries significant implications for the content, aims, and methods of teaching.

THEOLOGICAL ASSUMPTIONS AND IMPLICATIONS FOR EDUCATION

- God exists eternally and created humans to know, love, and glorify him. The ultimate purpose of education is to help learners to know, love, and glorify God.

- The Bible is the true Word of God given to human beings so that we can know and love him. Mastery and application of the Bible is the core curriculum.

- God created the world and everything in it. All of creation is open to study, and each academic discipline has the potential of promoting human development.

- All human beings are created in the image of God. Every individual has great worth and dignity, no matter their gender, ethnic background, or academic giftedness.

- Human beings will live forever. The purpose of education must not only equip students to be successful in this world but also to prepare them for eternity.

---

[3]Much of my education has been steeped in the theories of Jean Piaget, Lawrence Kohlberg, Erik Erikson, and similar developmentalists. While modern scholars have adapted and embellished their theories, I'm convinced that the core concepts of these developmentalists are helpful in understanding human development.

- All humans are fallen, with a natural tendency toward evil, so a radical child-centered education is not appropriate.

- Christ died for our sins to reconcile us to God and to our fellow human beings. While people apart from Christ can have many honorable qualities, they cannot fully develop into all God created them to become without forgiveness of sins through Christ.

- The Holy Spirit is the ultimate teacher and illuminates God's truth to students through his gifting of the teacher. It is important for teachers to pray that the Holy Spirit will work through their teaching. Skillful teaching is important yet still insufficient to promote godly growth.

- God established a community of believers, the church, for our nurture and for good in the world. Education must be both individual and communal, personal and corporate. The church is a means of God's grace to promote human development and love for God and others.

These are not radical theological assumptions: each is consistent with historic orthodox Christianity. In one sense, the teaching approach in this book challenges some present-day assumptions about schooling. But in a deeper sense, it is quite traditional, building on the observations of early Greek philosophers, the wisdom of the ancient Hebrews, the teaching of Jesus, and the insights of modern developmental educators. I'm convinced that effective innovation must be firmly rooted in traditional wisdom.

STILL LEARNING

In the complex arena of education and culture, I write as a learner, not as an expert. I could have titled the book "My 101 Greatest Mistakes in Teaching Across Cultures." I spent thirteen years serving under the leadership of the Evangelical Church Winning All (ECWA) in Nigeria, where I wrote curriculum and conducted seminars around the country.[4]

---

[4]The Nigerian denomination Evangelical Church Winning All (ECWA) used to be called the Evangelical Churches of West Africa. Today the denomination is one of the largest in Nigeria with over six thousand churches and about five million worshipers each Sunday. Today they

I was continually humbled by my limited ability to teach and write effectively in Africa. Later, I became the administrator for ECWA theological schools and again realized my need for a better understanding of Nigerian educational cultural values. My doctoral studies grew out of this sense of needing to understand culture and cognition more deeply.

Even after years of experience, I still feel my inadequacy every time I walk into a classroom of multicultural students. But I also teach and write as a curious learner who is growing from my mistakes, reflecting with deep joy when students take steps toward becoming all God intends them to be. No matter how many times I am privileged to facilitate this process, it still amazes me and renews my love for a life of teaching. Nothing could be more fulfilling.

MY LEARNING JOURNEY

Earlier I mentioned that effective teachers are intentionally mastering three things: the content to be taught, the culture of the learner, and the ability to encourage bridges between the content and the culture.

During my youth I never really understood the connection between academic studies and life. I played the education game. At church I won most of the Bible memory contests, but my motivation was to beat other kids in the youth group, not to grow in godliness.

In college my goal was to get the best grades possible with the least amount of effort. Like Mark Twain, I didn't want schooling to interfere with my education. I remember approaching my primary professor, Dr. Lois LeBar, and asking her only half-jokingly what I needed to do in the class in order to get a C. She almost wept. Again I didn't make a connection between the content of the course and my need to learn.

I failed the first quiz in an Old Testament survey course. For the second quiz I used a technique to memorize long lists by learning related acronyms. I also taught my roommate the technique. I got

---

have eleven Bible colleges and seminaries with fifteen theological training institutes. The denomination was started by the Sudan Interior Mission (now Serving in Mission or SIM), which began work in Nigeria in 1893.

100 percent on the second quiz and then promptly forgot the acronym five minutes after class. My roommate forgot the acronym five minutes before the quiz and got an F. So the difference between an A and an F was five minutes of memory.

All this changed when I arrived in Nigeria to serve as head of the Christian education department for the Evangelical Churches of West Africa, working with about one thousand churches at the time. I realized that much of my previous education did little to help me solve the challenges of education in Nigerian churches and schools. Most of the deficiency was mine in not making the connection between content and the practical needs of the church. Now I was desperate to understand how culture influenced the way people learned.

As a new missionary in Nigeria, I decided to observe a typical Sunday school class. I slipped into the back of a roomful of noisy children. At the end of the lesson, an elderly teacher stepped forward and announced, "Now it's time for a contest. Let us see who learned the lesson. The first question is, How many wives did Solomon have?" "Three hundred!" they shouted in unison. "Correct!" bellowed the teacher. "How many concubines did he have?" "Seven hundred!" they yelled. "Well done, children. You have learned your lesson. Class is dismissed." I was stunned. Polygamy was still a relevant dilemma in the churches, and no one, not the teacher, not the curriculum writer, and not the children saw any connection between the Bible and the concerns of Nigerian life. I doubt if any of the children had the slightest idea of the meaning of *concubine*. The irrelevance of the class pushed me to seek ways to help Nigerian learners see the connection between the Bible and life.

When we returned to the United States for a year, I decided to continue graduate education. At Wheaton Graduate School, Marvin Mayers opened my eyes to a powerful new world of basic cultural values. At Michigan State University, Ted Ward introduced me to research about the effects of culture on cognition. For the first time in my life, I felt genuinely excited about significant bodies of knowledge because they connected relevantly with my felt needs as an educator in Nigeria.

WHO NEEDS THIS BOOK?

The world is experiencing massive population shifts that affect us all. Millions of Africans, Asians, Latin Americans, and Middle Easterners have left their countries in search of safety, freedom, or economic survival. People with significant cultural differences are no longer hidden in far off, exotic countries but are at our doorstep in every continent. Many of our neighbors, friends, or work colleagues were born in another country. While such enormous population shifts trigger political challenges, they also provide an astounding opportunity for the growth of God's kingdom. To benefit from this opportunity, we must learn to engage people from many cultures.

I would be delighted if this book helped a Brazilian youth group leader serving in Miami, Koreans teaching in Bolivia, Ecuadorians coaching in India, pastors from Canada preaching in Vietnam, or Kenyans teaching in London.

I also hope the book will be helpful for professors who teach in classrooms of diverse students, both in their local cultures and globally. I trust it will be helpful for public school teachers, homeschoolers, and pastors, as well as camp counselors, mentors, parents, and grandparents, who, in an important sense, are teaching across cultures.

I earnestly pray that the ideas in this book will be used of the Lord for more effective teaching in making obedient disciples in all nations.

RELATIONAL TEACHING

By Giovani Pineda from Guatemala, teaching in Ethiopia, India, and the United States

As a Latino, my tendency in teaching is relational rather than a purely informational method. I like to walk through experiences with those I teach and then observe their reactions so that I can use those in further teaching.

In Ethiopia I took a team of seminary and university students to an unreached people group. I placed myself with the group in the village situation and watched them react. The Ethiopians reacted in different ways. Interestingly, those who were older and had been exposed to seminary teaching were having the most problems. Those who had not been exposed to Western styles of learning were more flexible and had less difficulty.

It is so much easier to teach when life is real. I find it difficult to teach theory in a classroom and much prefer to live the process with those who are learning with me. When teaching in other cultures, we have to be aware of our own learning and teaching styles as well as theirs. It also requires an understanding of Western influence in that culture.

In India, I partnered with a church-planting effort where there were many believers from Muslim backgrounds. I learned that Asians do their teaching through storytelling. Stories that reflected the realities of village life were the best. Of course, the Bible is full of really good stories, so focusing on those instead of dealing with the Bible as a textbook was important. In this case also, my Latin background pushed me to relational teaching, and it became important for me to experience village life firsthand.

Teaching Western-culture people is probably one of my most difficult tasks as a Latin because it requires a great deal of verbal precision and impressive use of facts. If it were not for the grace of the Spirit of God, it is almost impossible to calm myself and be able to teach in English with Western people. In my culture, words don't carry the same amount of weight as they do in English because we speak indirectly and almost in a circular style. So to become direct and fact-oriented is nerve-racking! I do it for the glory of God and by his grace.

1

METAPHORS OF TEACHING

Anyone who listens to my teaching and follows it is wise,
like a person who builds a house on solid rock.

Matthew 7:24 NLT

If you are planning for a year, sow rice: if you are planning for
a decade, plant trees; if you are planning for a lifetime, teach people.

Chinese Proverb

Ted Ward was a popular and successful classroom teacher at
Michigan State University, but his most significant teaching probably took
place outside the classroom. He often invited his doctoral students to his
home for integrative discussions. On one occasion he invited me to travel
with him, where I observed him teaching a faculty workshop at another
university. On the long drive home, we debriefed what happened at the
workshop. Ted taught me important concepts formally and informally,
always concerned about my personal and intellectual development.

What makes a teacher effective? What kind of teaching promotes
human development? In this chapter we'll look at metaphors for understanding our subconscious cultural expectations about teaching. Ted
Ward often spoke of the power of metaphors in our teaching. He complained that the most common metaphors in teaching were those of
filling a container or education as a manufacturing process.[1] He argued
that learners are neither blank slates nor raw material. He observes,

---

[1]Ted W. Ward, "Evaluating Metaphors of Education," in *With an Eye on the Future: Development and Mission in the 21st Century: Essays in Honor of Ted Ward*, ed. Duane Elmer and Lois McKin-ney (Monrovia, CA: MARC, 1996), 46.

Teachers who think of education in terms of filling a container are rarely concerned with individual differences of the background, interest or aspiration. The *content* is the thing. Most learning can be reduced to questions and answers; recall of information is the evidence of becoming educated; tests are good indicators of "success" or "failure"; grading can be objective. The more the teacher knows, the better the teacher is. Learning is essentially painful, but it is such good discipline! Such thinking leads to teaching that is little more than cognitive dumping.[2]

Ted Ward also built on the metaphors of Herbert M. Kliebard, the distinguished professor of education at the University of Wisconsin–Madison, who developed the educational metaphors of *production*, *growth*, and *travel*.[3] His metaphors have become classic examples of a mindset regarding what we value in teaching. As I've written previously, "Metaphors are often unconscious, or at least not clearly defined in our minds. Yet these hidden pictures predispose us to be attracted to certain methods of Christian education and to be suspicious of others. Metaphors are an indication of inner values."[4] Metaphors about teaching are often below the level of our awareness and are sometimes accepted uncritically as the normal way to teach.

Production: The teacher as technician. In this metaphor, "the curriculum is the means of production, and the student is the raw material which will be transformed into a finished and useful product under the control of a highly skilled technician."[5] The educational objective for teachers who see themselves as highly skilled technicians is uniformity, efficiency, and predictability.

Growth: The teacher as gardener. In the growth metaphor, "the curriculum is the greenhouse where students will grow and develop to their fullest potential under the care of a wise and patient gardener. The plants that grow in the greenhouse are of every variety, but the

---

[2]Ward, "Evaluating Metaphors," 47.
[3]Herbert M. Kliebard. "Metaphorical Roots of Curriculum Design," in *Curriculum Theorizing: The Reconceptualists*, ed. William Pinar (Richmond, CA: McCutchan Publishing, 1975), 84-85.
[4]James E. Plueddemann, "Metaphors in Christian Education," *Christian Education Journal* 7, no. 1 (1986): 40.
[5]Plueddemann, "Metaphors in Christian Education," 84.

gardener treats each according to its needs so that each plant comes to flower."[6] The educational aim of the gardener is opposite to that of the highly skilled technician. The goal of the gardener is for students to blossom in whatever way their nature inclines them to grow. This process is not uniform, efficient, or predictable.

Travel: The teacher as tour guide. In this metaphor, "the curriculum is a route over which students will travel under the leadership of an experienced guide and companion. Each traveler will be affected differently by the journey since its effect is at least as much a function of the predilections, intelligence, interests and intent of the traveler as it is of the contours of the route."[7] The aim of the tour guide is to provide "a journey as rich, as fascinating, and as memorable as possible"[8] for student travelers.

All three metaphors have an educational following, and all three have strengths and weaknesses. The metaphor of *production* ignores the context of the learner. The *growth* metaphor focuses almost exclusively on the context of the learner. The *travel* metaphor considers both the information to be learned and the context of the learner, but lacks a clear sense of destination.

In his classic book *The Third Wave*, Alvin Toffler argues that during the Industrial Revolution the *production* model was dominant. The purpose of school was to prepare children to work in factories.[9] The explicit curriculum was reading, writing, and arithmetic, but the hidden curriculum was to prepare children for the assembly line by teaching them to be punctual, obedient, and able to do repetitive work.[10] Schooling was seen as an *assembly line*. Factory workers needed to come to work on time and take orders from management without questioning. The school became an ideal means for preparing humans to do repetitious operations, much like robots.

The three metaphors reflect cultural values. According to the highly regarded anthropologist Edward T. Hall, most cultures of the world

---

[6]Plueddemann, "Metaphors in Christian Education," 84.
[7]Plueddemann, "Metaphors in Christian Education," 85.
[8]Plueddemann, "Metaphors in Christian Education," 85.
[9]Alvin Toffler, *The Third Wave* (New York: Bantam Books, 1980), 29.
[10]Toffler, *Third Wave*, 29.

are more attuned to the *environment* or the context, whereas *words* carry more meaning than the context in my northern European cultural heritage.[11] We often assume that schooling is made up of decontextualized ideas and abstract theories. We may assume context is extraneous, but for most cultures the context communicates even more than verbal content. In these cultures, nonverbal signals embedded in the environment—the expressiveness of the teacher, the body language of students, and classroom seating arrangement are loaded with meaning and can communicate even more information than mere words.

It's ironic that because of globalization, schooling around the world now frequently follows the *production* or factory model even in cultures that traditionally emphasized the context of the learners or the *growth* metaphor. The combination of the production model of teaching carried out in cultures with a value of high power distance between the teacher and the student is a challenge for real learning.

It's interesting to note that much educational research assumes a factory model and seeks to improve efficiency of the transfer of content rather than exploring the implications of education in the context of the student. No wonder the clash of global cultural values puts schooling in high demand while devaluing the importance of actual learning.

Understanding one's own teaching metaphor as well as that of the learner is imperative for the crosscultural teacher. Otherwise, disappointment and maybe even chaos will take place. One of my American friends taught for many years at a theological seminary in Africa. When students asked him a question, he gave them ideas for how they could look up the information for themselves. He wanted to help them learn how to learn, while the students assumed his role was to give them answers. The teacher decided that the students were immature, and the students thought the teacher was not very competent. This is a classic case of the conflict of expectations. The students expected a production professor, and the professor taught from a gardener metaphor.

---

[11]Edward T. Hall, *Beyond Culture* (Garden City, NY: Anchor Books, 1997), 91.

A PILGRIM TEACHING PILGRIMS

As I've taught around the world, I've struggled to find a metaphor that would be somewhat familiar in a variety of cultures and yet incorporate my convictions about the importance of integrating God-given bodies of knowledge with the existential needs of learners. The metaphor I've come to develop over several decades, inspired by *Pilgrim's Progress* by John Bunyan, is that of *pilgrimage.*

Every culture of the world has stories of journeys and treks, sojourns and voyages. The narrative of pilgrimage is embedded in our human psyche and finds expression in the libraries and folklore of almost all cultures.

In this metaphor, both students and teacher are pilgrims together in the learning journey. The pilgrim teacher may have more experience on the path and greater knowledge of map reading, but teacher and students are fellow travelers, and pilgrim students have much to contribute to the journey.

My hunch is that different cultures prefer certain metaphors of teaching. The strength of the pilgrim metaphor is that it is flexible enough to fit into a wide variety of cultures. It builds on the strengths of the three Kliebard metaphors while it seeks to overcome the weakness of each. The strength of the teacher as technician is that it takes seriously the subject matter to be taught. Unfortunately, it tends to downplay the context of the learner. The strength of the teacher as gardener is that it takes seriously the needs and interests of individual learners, but places little emphasis on subject matter. The teacher as tour guide may seem similar to the pilgrim metaphor, emphasizing the richness of the journey. But the travel metaphor assumes that a tourist's primary need is experiences, not development.

The metaphor of *pilgrimage* incorporates all three elements of Kliebard's metaphors. Because pilgrims need information, there are aspects of *production*. Parts of the *gardener* metaphor are also helpful as pilgrim teachers focus on the development of uniquely gifted pilgrims, equipping and strengthening them for the journey. My best teachers were *tour guides* who taught with a pilgrim mindset both in and out of the classroom.

All of us are on a journey with an eternal destination. As Bunyan describes it, our ultimate objective is the celestial city, and our secondary goal is to make progress in the journey. From a biblical perspective, the ultimate outcome of teaching is to help the learner to love the Lord with all one's heart, soul, and strength (Deut 6:5). The secondary aim is to promote the development of the pilgrim until we all attain "the whole measure of the fullness of Christ" (Eph 4:13). In this eternal perspective, the most important educational objectives will not be completely fulfilled in this lifetime. So the pilgrim metaphor runs counter to the factory metaphor. Pilgrim teachers don't see students as raw material to be molded into identical products in the most efficient and time-effective manner.

In the pilgrim metaphor, the mastery of knowledge is important, yet it is not the ultimate outcome. The task of mastering bodies of information is a necessary *means* not an *end*. Pilgrims should diligently learn the art of the compass and conscientiously study the map. But they don't master these skills merely to gain multiple map certificates that will lead to high-paying jobs. Advanced studies in the field of map reading and research into new compass design are valued because they enrich the journey of pilgrims. Such studies lead to the development of pilgrims when connected to the experiences of the road.

Near the beginning of the journey described by Bunyan, the main character, Christian, spends time in Interpreter's house, where he learns lessons of theology to help him on the path. He is given a scroll and instructions about the dangers ahead.

We are given the map of the Bible, God's supernatural communication to pilgrims and the instruction book for the journey of life. And through God's general revelation we are given an astonishing variety of insightful academic disciplines. A true understanding of the sciences, humanities, and social sciences helps us to understand ourselves, our neighbor, and God. The pilgrim metaphor respects academic rigor while focusing on the development of pilgrims as they travel toward their ultimate purpose in life.

Pilgrims travel together. Learners need the individual skills of each member of the pilgrim band in order to equip one another for the journey. Pilgrims lift one another up when fallen and put their arm around the shoulder of the learner who is ready to quit. One pilgrim may have individual strengths in reading maps, another skills in rock climbing, and another sharp eyes to see far up the road. Individuals use their skills for strengthening one another.

This metaphor integrates the strengths of both individualistic and collectivistic cultures without caving to the weaknesses of either. Strongly individualistic cultures tend to produce egotistical, self-centered people. Intensely collectivistic cultures may stifle creativity and the development of individuals. Either extreme can lead to dehumanization and can be harmful to society.

I enjoy teaching university students in the classroom, but I value with equal pleasure the times spent in my office listening to their stories and praying with them. When I taught at Wheaton College in Illinois, my wife and I invited students and their friends to our home on Sunday evenings for food and friendship. In our living room, we listened to the stories of fellow pilgrims who shared the joys and sorrows of their journey, and we prayed for one another. These times were rich learning experiences for all of us.

Teachers who demonstrate the power of pilgrim teaching use a combination of *production*, *growth*, and *travel* metaphors. In isolation, the metaphors are dysfunctional. The *production* metaphor by itself assumes students are empty heads that need filling. I often call this the *factory* metaphor. The *growth* metaphor by itself develops narcissistic, self-centered students, growing into isolated individualists. I sometimes refer to this as the *wildflower* approach—just let students bloom as they wish. The *tour guide* metaphor is also inadequate by itself in that it sees students as tourists instead of purposeful pilgrims. The tour guide desires to make the journey rich and fascinating, with no sense of a destination or purpose. By themselves the three Kliebard metaphors are insufficient, but combined in a pilgrim metaphor they promote the journey of human development with an ultimate destination and a compelling purpose for living.

The pilgrim metaphor is useful in multicultural settings as it incorporates the importance of both the practical and the academic.

FROM KOREA TO ECUADOR

By Felipe Byun, Global Missionary Training Center, Korea

Teaching and living in Ecuador broadened my limited perspective on theology and the Christian life.

As a product of the Korean church, I was influenced greatly by evangelical pietism and puritanism. I didn't have sufficient appreciation for the aesthetic and ritualistic aspects of Christian teaching. We studied the Bible in a similar way to students studying their subjects in a classroom setting. This probably reflected the influence of Confucianism, which put importance on the study of sacred books.

In Ecuador, however, I observed the Catholics effectively using celebrations and religious fiestas as a context for teaching. As a result, I started to deliberately emphasize the special events of the church calendar in the congregation I led. For Palm Sunday, we decorated our church entrance with palm branches. We made special colorful pendants to remind us of Lent, Resurrection Sunday, Pentecost, Advent, and Christmas.

From Latino Communion services, I learned an important aspect of the biblical meaning of Communion that had been invisible in Korean Communion services. Communion is a foretaste of the coming fiesta of the Lamb!

My experience in Ecuador helped me understand that there can be diverse methods of effective teaching in various cultural contexts.

2

THE RAIL FENCE AS A CROSSCULTURAL MODEL FOR TEACHING

How can a young person stay on the path of purity?
By living according to your word.

PSALM 119:9

IT SEEMS OBVIOUS that in addition to teaching content, the educator's task in any situation is to help students make connections between the subject matter and their experience. The educational model I've used in teaching across cultures is that of the rail fence.[1] The top rail represents the subject matter: Scripture, the academic disciplines, or other bodies of knowledge. The bottom rail represents the needs, interests, culture, and struggles of the learner. The responsibility of the teacher doesn't end with teaching content and relating it to the life experience. It's also to help students build fence posts between the subject matter and their needs. Only the learner can truly make the personal application, though the teacher should facilitate the connection. The fence posts signify the interface between theory and practice. They represent the connecting links between truth and life, tying together

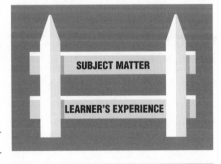

Figure 2.1. The rail-fence educational model

[1]James E. Plueddemann, "The Disease of the Sunday School: Rail Fence Analogy for Curriculum Design," *Evangelical Missions Quarterly* 7, no. 2 (1972): 88-92. I first became aware of the rail-fence model from Ted Ward during his visit to Nigeria in 1971, and I adapted it for the Sunday school. As far as I know I was the first person to publish the model.

the needs and interests of the learner with bodies of knowledge capable of addressing the learner's reality. The fence posts hold together the fruitful tension between truth and life (see fig. 2.1).

The Rail Fence from Scripture

Understanding and obeying God's Word is a dominant theme in all of Scripture. The rail-fence model mirrors this biblical emphasis.

The model is really as old as Adam and Eve (see fig. 2.2). God began with the bottom-rail experience of being in the Garden of Eden with trees "pleasing to the eye and good for food" (Gen 2:9). Then God gave them the top-rail command to be fruitful and multiply (Gen 1:28), and charged them not to eat from the tree of the knowledge of good and evil (Gen 2:17). The serpent challenged God's command and their need to obey it (Gen 3:1). Adam and Eve disobeyed God, ignoring the needed connection between God's command and their actions (Gen 3:6-7).

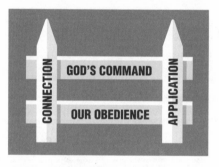

Figure 2.2. The rail-fence and the creation story

Moses continually pled with Israel to "walk in obedience to all that the LORD your God has commanded you" (Deut 5:33a). Walking in obedience was the bottom-rail application, and the commands of God were the top-rail subject matter. Moses begged his people not just to make the intellectual connection between God's commands and their lives, but to make the connection in such a way that would promote their development "so that you may live and prosper and prolong your days in the land that you will possess" (Deut 5:33b).

Probably Moses's most compelling teaching is found in Deuteronomy 6. He begins with the bottom rail by promising long life in a land flowing with milk and honey (Deut 6:1-3). He then challenges Israel with some of the most important subject matter in the Bible: "Hear, O Israel: The LORD our God, the LORD is one. Love the LORD your God with all your heart and with all your soul and with all your strength" (Deut 6:4-5). The rest of the passage commands parents to teach this truth to their children with bottom-rail teaching methods. Parents are to impress these truths on children in the context of daily life—talking about them in the home, when going to bed, and with reminders on their foreheads and all around the house (Deut 6:6-9). Moses began with the bottom rail of long life and a land flowing with milk and honey. Then he taught top-rail theology about the nature of God and the purpose of life. He then entreated parents to help their children make the connection between the two in the everyday experiences of life.

Parents can teach and encourage application, but they can't guarantee fence-post connections. Their children need to make the connection for themselves.

All 176 verses in Psalm 119 reflect the rail-fence model. Psalm 119:105 describes it well: "Your word [top rail] is a lamp for my feet, / a light on my path [bottom rail]." Verse 1 describes the fence-post application. "Blessed are those whose ways are blameless, / who walk according to the law of the LORD."

Jesus' teachings consistently reflected the need to connect truth and life. Consider the stories of the wise man who built his house on a rock, the farmer who sowed seed on different soils, the prodigal son who returned to his father.

Paul pled for unity between Jews and Gentiles in his letter to the Romans. He addressed factions between those were weak in faith and those who were strong. He dealt with bottom-rail practical problems in light of top-rail theology, profoundly connecting the two. Paul often pleaded with believers to build fence posts by putting into practice the teachings of Scripture (Rom 12:1-2; Phil 4:2).

James reminds believers that top-rail knowledge is inadequate. Even the demons believe in one God (Jas 2:19). True top-rail faith must be reflected in bottom-rail works (Jas 2:17). "As the body without the spirit is dead, so faith without works is dead" (James 2:26; see fig. 2.3).

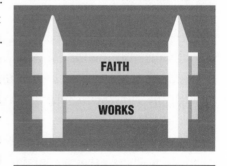

Figure 2.3. Connecting faith and works

Objections to the Rail-Fence Model

I was finishing a day-long seminar on the rail-fence model with a group of curriculum editors. I began with bottom-rail examples from their current Sunday school curriculum and taught interactively all day about biblical, theological, and educational principles. Just as we were about to dismiss the seminar, one editor in the back announced that he wasn't convinced by my teaching. He challenged me with Hebrews 4:12: "The word of God is alive and active. Sharper than any double-edged sword." He then quoted Isaiah 55:11, "So is my word that goes out from my mouth: / It will not return to me empty." He concluded that the curriculum merely needed to teach the Bible and let the Bible speak for itself.

I was discouraged, feeling that my inadequate teaching had bungled an outstanding opportunity to influence significant editors. Later as I re-read the context of the Hebrews and Isaiah passages I realized that neither passage suggested an automatic connection between the Word of God and godly living. The Hebrews 4 passage is in the context of a warning about not entering the Sabbath rest. The top-rail message they heard was of no value to them because they didn't connect the Word with the bottom rail of obedience (Heb 4:2).

Likewise the Isaiah 55 passage affirms that God's Word "will not return empty," but it goes on to say it "will accomplish what I desire / and achieve the purpose for which I sent it" (v. 11). In the same chapter Isaiah pleads with Israel to "Let the wicked forsake their ways / and the unrighteous their thoughts" (Is 55:7). The Word of God will accomplish its purpose of either judgment or blessing. Isaiah challenged the people to connect the bottom rail of their wicked ways with the top rail of God's promises for mercy and pardon (v. 7).

Of course there are times when the living and active Word of God, through the Holy Spirit, makes an application to our deepest needs. Unfortunately, though, many of us apply only a tiny fraction of what we know of Scripture to everyday living. Like Isaiah and the writer of Hebrews, teachers need to communicate the Word of God and plead with learners to put it into practice.

IMPLICATIONS FOR TEACHING

Effective teaching should normally begin with the bottom-rail culture, felt needs, and experiences of the students. The teacher then presents top-rail bodies of information that have the potential of connecting with the learners' experience. The teacher can hint at fence posts, but ultimately the connection needs to be made by the students through the power of the Holy Spirit.

The rail fence is a reflection of the pilgrim metaphor. As pilgrims begin to overcome personal challenges on their journey by following the map of God's truth, they make progress on the journey. They progress through a learning cycle of bottom-rail struggles and top-rail solutions, connecting the two fence posts. Each cycle brings the pilgrim closer to maturity (see fig. 2.4).

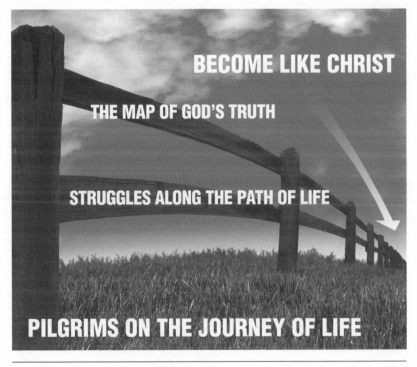

Figure 2.4. Progress through the learning cycle

THE DANGER OF DISCONNECTION

It is dangerous to disconnect the world of ideas from the practical, to divorce schooling from life. Too often educators assume that the role of schooling is to transmit subject matter that is disconnected from life.

In much of the world we see an emphasis on standardized testing. Such testing measures how much students know from predetermined information while ignoring the real world of students. It does not take into account the home life, neighborhood, or language ability of students. Its purpose is to provide a uniform standard to measure the mastery of prescribed knowledge for a wide range of students, regardless of their context. While standardized tests have a role in education, the fact that they intentionally ignore the student's context means their usefulness is limited.

An article in the *New York Times* describes Public School 188 on the Lower East Side of Manhattan. It points out the problem of neglecting the context, where half the pupils are homeless.

> Since school began in September, five new students have arrived and eight children have left. Two transferred out in November. One who started in January was gone in April. A boy showed up for a single day in March, and then never came back. Even now, in the twilight of the school year, new students are still arriving, one as recently as mid-May.[2]

The teachers at Public School 188 are trying to improve test scores in the context of students who live in foster homes, on the street, or with eleven people in a small one-room apartment. On any given day, Principal Suany Ramos might "welcome two or three new students and watch one disappear."[3] While only 9 percent of the students meet state standards in English, Ms. Ramos measures success by how much the school has done for families. This story is a fascinating example of a formal school attempting to meet the situational needs of the family while working hard to raise context-independent test scores.

---

[2]Elizabeth A. Harris, "Where Nearly Half of Pupils Are Homeless, School Aims to Be Teacher, Therapist, Even Santa," *New York Times*, June 6, 2016, www.nytimes.com/2016/06/07/nyregion /public-school-188-in-manhattan-about-half-the-students-are-homeless.html.
[3]Harris, "Where Nearly Half of Pupils Are Homeless."

Theological schools often struggle with the same separation of content and context, with no integrating fence posts. Most courses in Bible and theology reflect the historical scholarship of the ages while ignoring the theological pitfalls of the modern church. Of course students must study the writings of past scholars in order to understand the challenges of the present, but not many professors or students make the practical connection.

I once consulted with a theological school in the Democratic Republic of the Congo, reviewing their curriculum to help them gain accreditation. They taught a top-rail theology course on soteriology (the doctrine of salvation) and a bottom-rail practical course on personal evangelism. The soteriology professor was appalled when he observed one of his students in the local market advocating a heretical view of salvation while he fulfilled an evangelism course requirement. The school realized that the curriculum offered a *balance* between practical and theoretical courses, but there was little *integration* of the two. Of course many outstanding theology professors constantly integrate theology with life, and Congolese school worked hard to do this more intentionally.

Several years ago I conducted a two-day doctoral seminar for American seminary students on how to teach. They were about to graduate and become professors. I began the morning with the factory-production model, drawing an assembly line on the blackboard. It was a model of "teach them, test them, and graduate them." At the break time, several students thanked me for such a good model of teaching. They felt there were many things they could use as future professors. I begged them to hold off their evaluation until the end of the seminar. In the afternoon I taught the pilgrim metaphor using the rail-fence approach. At the end of that session, the same students again thanked me for the presentation. They agreed that the pilgrim model was better than the factory model. Then one student asked, "If the pilgrim model is the best model, how come I've almost never experienced it in our seminary?"

Adult Sunday school classes face the same dilemma. In our church, we offer at least two classes, one a content-heavy course and the other a more practical course. We might offer bottom-rail classes on marriage or evangelism, and top-rail classes on Ephesians or Reformed distinctives. We struggle to build integrating fence posts.

Preaching styles often follow a similar pattern. Some top-rail preachers exposit a book of the Bible verse by verse, ending the sermon with only a minute or two for a vague application. Bottom-rail pastors preach on practical topics of real-world interest to the congregation. They may refer to a few Bible references, but the emphasis is on the practical, not the theological. Only seldom are the two rails tied together in a consistently life-changing way.

The main problem in education worldwide is the lack of integration between ideas and practice, between truth and life, between the biblical content and cultural context. Both rails are necessary, but neither is sufficient. Effective teaching is transformational when teachers challenge students to make connections between the rails.

HELPING KOREAN THIRD-CULTURE KIDS TO THRIVE

By Ruth Baek, Global Missionary Training Center, Korea

The educational environment for Korean Third-Culture Kids (TCKs) is far better today than in the early 1980s and 1990s, when the Korean mission movement rapidly expanded. Both overseas schools and Korean communities have gained more understanding about each other's culture, needs, and expectations. But there are still great challenges. Some of these challenges are bilingual issues; others are learning to hold cherished cultural values in tension with differences in educational philosophy and methodology. There can also be a lack of communication between parents and teachers due to language and cultural barriers.

Lack of English proficiency intermingled with cultural, social, and relational issues can lead to low self-esteem and sometimes to psychological depression. When it comes to a power language like English, the teacher's cultural prejudice and insensitivity can often make students feel inferior and discriminated against.

It is important for those who teach crossculturally to understand second-language issues so they can lend support and encouragement to students. Minority students who come from another country will greatly appreciate a teacher who shows respect and openness to learn their culture and to affirm them for who they are. This will give students courage to overcome the challenges they face and help them to be a source of blessing for the whole school community. They will bring richness to the learning community not only by their strengths but also by their weaknesses. Learning how to harmonize cultural differences will be a great education for those who live in this global era and will reflect what the kingdom of God looks like.

As TCKs from many countries face the challenges of diversity, they will learn together to become bridge builders in our globalized world.

3

ADAPTING OUR COLORED GLASSES

The world is a book and those who do not travel read only one page.
AUGUSTINE OF HIPPO

The whole purpose of teaching is to turn mirrors into windows.
SIDNEY J. HARRIS

WHY IS IT THAT TEACHERS who are successful at home are often ineffective in another culture? Is it possible that being a great teacher in one context may lead to overconfidence, making it *more difficult* to be flexible or to change gears and connect with learners who have different cultural expectations? The very skills that make a teacher effective in one culture may make it more challenging to be effective in another.

A new missionary from the United States was asked to teach a course on marriage and the family at a Nigerian seminary. Students were attentive and seemed to appreciate his dynamic teaching, but halfway through the semester a student said, "Sir, thank you so much for this excellent class, but please explain one thing: *What is dating?*" My friend confessed that he had simply used his seminary notes from the United States to teach the same course in a Nigerian seminary without pausing to inquire about the nature of marriage and family in Nigeria. This professor was an outstanding teacher in the United States, and he eventually adjusted well to the Nigerian culture. What was the problem? It wasn't a lack of appreciation for the host culture but the hidden assumption that education consists in transferring information from the professor to the student, so that in some mysterious way the content will be practical to the learner.

One of my university professor friends half-jokingly remarked, "Often teaching is transferring information from the notes of the professor to the notes of the student without going through the head of either one." Effective teaching demands that the teacher be as well versed in the learner's culture as in the subject matter. *To be a teacher of students, one must first be a student of students.* The key problem for many crosscultural teachers is assuming that their subject matter expertise can be transmitted to their students without taking into account the context and cultural values of the learner. These teachers need a paradigm shift.

WHY A PARADIGM SHIFT?

A few hundred years ago most people could go through life without ever meeting a stranger. Everyone knew everyone else in their village, and most were related at some level. Assumptions about *why* to teach, *who* should teach, *what* should be taught, and *how* and *where* to teach were subconsciously understood by everyone. Most teaching was in the practical context of the community. Everyone for miles around knew the educational assumptions and took them for granted.[1]

Charlie and David Davis of TEAM recounted a story that happened after the 2005 earthquake in the Himalayan mountain range of Pakistan. After the initial rescue operations, workers moved into a community development phase. Traditionally farmers scattered their seed. The experts knew that if farmers planted the seed corn instead of scattering it, it would germinate much better. The community development workers found a plot of ground to demonstrate their ideas, and, indeed, the plot generated many more bushels of corn than did the scatter method. When a local farmer was asked if he would change his method, he shrugged in a noncommittal way. When asked why he didn't want to change, he cited history and practice. Conformity to

---

[1]Edward T. Hall, *Beyond Culture* (Garden City, NY: Anchor Books, 1997), 41.

their traditional way of doing things was of far more value to him than the pragmatic value of producing more corn. It took hours of sitting in the local tea shops developing relationships and understanding what farmers valued before launching the new method. Later, as local farmers observed the results of the new seed-planting methods, some began to increase their yield with the new method. The development effort was eventually successful as the workers connected cultural values with scientific research.

A true agricultural expert must first listen to the local farmers, honor their efforts, and observe their practices. Only then should they make suggestions from their own expertise. This principle can be expanded to all teaching and is urgently appropriate in teaching across cultures.

In our globalizing world, the importance of figuring out how to teach across cultures is more crucial than ever. We need a paradigm shift that connects information with the life and cultural values of the learner.

Paradigms are ways of seeing. Stephen Covey writes,

> The word *paradigm* comes from the Greek. It was originally a scientific term, and is more commonly used today to mean a model, theory, perception, assumption, or frame of reference. In the more general sense, it's the way we "see" the world—not in terms of our visual sense of sight, but in terms of perceiving, understanding, interpreting.[2]

Paradigms might be described as the culturally defined colored glasses that influence the way we see the world. The difficulty is that we assume everyone sees the world as we do, not recognizing that people in different cultures perceive the world through glasses of different colors. When people begin to teach across cultures, the assumption that everyone sees the world like me leads to frustration.

WHAT IS A PARADIGM SHIFT?

I remember an experience in ninth grade when a friend allowed me to look through his glasses. I was stunned. I had no idea that trees at a distance could be so clear. I only knew that everything more than

---

[2]Stephen R. Covey, *The Seven Habits of Highly Effective People: Powerful Lessons in Personal Change* (New York: Simon & Schuster, 1989), 32.

six feet away was fuzzy, and I assumed fuzziness was normal. I almost failed high school geometry because I couldn't see the shapes and angles on the blackboard during the exam. Even when the teacher allowed me to sit in the front row, I could barely make out the triangles and trapezoids. I needed eyeglasses.

Likewise, people who teach in only one culture must put on different glasses for teaching in another. Unfortunately, these teachers may be unaware that the other culture has different perspectives about the learner, the purpose of education, and the best ways to teach.

Visualize a town where students attend school primarily to pass exams. Their motive is to be accepted into prestigious schools and eventually to secure high-paying jobs. They've been taught that rote learning is the best way to pass an exam. Teachers and students work well together because they are wearing identical glasses.

Then imagine that a teacher arrives from another part of the world with different-colored glasses. The new teacher's paradigm is to challenge students to think, to wrestle with ideas and apply them to their context. The students and the teacher are wearing very different glasses but are unaware of the dissimilarities. The new teacher will likely be frustrated when students continually ask, "Will this be on the exam?" Students may even complain to the principal that the teacher is wasting valuable time with class discussions. The students may feel that the outside teacher is incompetent and isn't preparing them to pass exams in order to gain credentials and to obtain high-paying jobs. Cultural paradigms unconsciously influence both the content and method of teaching as well as the motivation for learning.

THE DIPLOMA DISEASE

Ronald Dore's classic book titled *The Diploma Disease* describes the disconnect between diplomas and economic development.[3] When the only purpose of schooling is to gain a diploma in order to get a job, the inflation of credentials is inevitable. An educational system that

---

[3]Ronald Dore, *The Diploma Disease: Education, Qualification and Development* (London: Institute of Education of London, 1997), 6.

merely equips students to pass exams does not lead to economic development or even the development of the student. Dore describes situations in India where because of the inflation of qualifications, thousands of graduate engineers earn a living by driving taxies. Dore also gives examples of Kenyan bus companies requiring a university degree to get a job as a bus conductor.[4]

Merely teaching for the test produces meaningless diplomas for pseudo-educated, unemployed graduates. Dore makes this case from examples and statistics in England, Japan, Sri Lanka, and Kenya. Preparing students to pass standardized tests in order to climb the schooling ladder in order to earn more money is anti-educational and actually hinders economic development. In many parts of the world, the diploma disease continues as a sickness.

A Ghanaian writer recently reported about massive cheating on exams in Ghana, Kenya, Zambia, and Zimbabwe.[5] Teachers, parents, and students were all involved in the leakage of exam questions. The parents' only worry was that schools in the United Kingdom and the United States would discover the cheating. It seemed all right to have worthless and degraded certificates as long as schools overseas didn't find out. The solution is not for more security on the exam, although that would be a good idea. The solution is a paradigm shift on the purpose of education.

The *Guardian* reported that twenty-five thousand Liberian students took the entrance exam for the University of Liberia with zero students passing. The article suggested that unlike previous years, to eliminate cheating, the school hired a private consultant to manage the exam.[6] The consultant observed, "There is a perception in our society that once you take the University of Liberia admissions exam, if you do not pay money to someone, or if you do not have appropriate connections, you would not be placed on the results list."[7]

---

[4]Dore, *Diploma Disease*, 6.

[5]Elizabeth Ohene, "Letter from Africa: Ghana's Exam Cheat Scandal," BBC, April 18, 2016, www .bbc.com/news/world-africa-36045607.

[6]David Smith, "All 25,000 Candidates Fail Liberian University Entrance Exam," *Guardian*, August 27, 2013.

[7]Smith, "All 25,000 Candidates Fail."

A paradigm shift is not a gradual improvement or a slight tweaking of an old way of doing things. It's not made up of small, incremental steps toward improvement, but is a radical reshaping of an understanding of teaching and learning. A butterfly isn't just a bigger caterpillar. An automobile is not just a better horse. The printing press is not a clever upgrade of a pencil. A paradigm shift is a metamorphosis, a transformation. In education, it's a fundamental change in the underlying assumptions about teaching and learning.

Making improvements to a wrong paradigm only makes things worse. Stephen Covey uses the illustration of a map to understand this concept.[8] It is useless to improve our map-reading skills if we have the wrong map. No matter how proficient I am at reading maps, using a map of Bogotá while trying to find my way around Quito will lead to massive frustration. Covey also uses the metaphor of a ladder. Ladder-climbing skills are useless if my ladder is leaning against the wrong wall. Seeking to tweak the old educational paradigm is just as senseless. We will simply become better and better at accomplishing the unimportant.

I suggest that the educational pilgrim model is often at odds with the dominant global paradigms today. Yet the pilgrim metaphor draws wisdom from some of the great educators throughout history and from biblical patterns. You've probably experienced this model in great teachers who have influenced you the most. I contend that the pilgrim metaphor is neither old nor new; it is timeless.

I'm convinced that the paradigm I'm suggesting has the potential of promoting effective teaching in any culture. It begins with students immersed in their cultural context and a teacher who helps the learners to tie together knowledge and life.

Have you ever walked in to an optometrist's shop for an eye exam and seen a glass case with dozens and dozens of glasses displayed? Each rim is a different color and shape, different pattern and size. And inside each frame will go a unique kind of glass—glass that will help its wearers see their surroundings with perfect clarity and sharpness. Good

---

[8]Covey, *Seven Habits of Highly Effective People*, 23.

teachers—those who can teach to anyone, anywhere—will have such a case of glasses in their mind. They will have acquired them over time after careful study of their students' cultures and values. These teachers, as much as possible, will modify the color of their glasses to better match those of their students in a different culture.

DEEP LISTENING AND RESPECT

By Diana Garrett from Costa Rica and Mirna Sotomayor from Mexico

We have been working with the Nahuatl (Aztec) people since 2009. Rather than doing the teaching ourselves, we have mostly facilitated Mestizo Mexicans to equip these indigenous Mexicans. By far the biggest obstacle is the barrier between the Mestizo and the Aztec. The Aztec regards the Mestizo with a mixture of fear and a deep sense of inferiority, rooted in the Spanish conquest over the Native peoples in the Americas.

Tensions have been relieved and deeper learning has been achieved with these guidelines:

- We respect and affirm the oral nature of the Aztec people. Learning is almost 100 percent oral and must be mediated by a native Aztec to get through.

- Native Aztecs are given authority not only to teach themselves but to transform the content, even if it does not look similar to the original. This is not easy because local leaders often deem it necessary to parrot the "superior" culture.

- The Mestizo Mexican teacher practices deep listening and truly values the positive aspects of the indigenous culture. The barrier of fear and inferiority is only broken by many hours of listening and listening and listening some more. We press ourselves into listening beyond what is considered reasonable and try not to lead the conversation. When we allow ourselves to be taken through an endless labyrinth of storytelling, suddenly the curtain will be lifted and we will be allowed to see deeply into the culture. This is how our Aztec friends perceive unconditional love.

- Give the whole indigenous community the opportunity to have direct contact with the Word of God, unmediated and uninterpreted by anyone other than the Holy Spirit. This is so hard, but not negotiable.

TEACHING COMPLEX CREATURES

*You never really understand a person until you consider things
from his point of view . . . until you climb into his skin
and walk around in it.*

Atticus Finch

There must be dozens of definitions of *culture*. But each definition reflects the same concept: culture describes characteristics that are *shared* by a *group* of people in behaviors, assumptions, beliefs, and values. The culture of a community makes an important impact on language, gender roles, child rearing, business practices, housing styles, clothing preferences, and food. Cultural values provide the structure for how people get along with each other, how they relate to their environment, how they think, feel, and behave. The influence of culture pervades every aspect of life. Even though a globalized world is becoming more homogenized, people continue to passionately protect local cultural values. It seems that both globalization and localization are becoming stronger at the same time.

In one course I taught, several of the students objected to the idea of stereotyping people by culture. They argued that each person is different, and it's wrong to relegate people into cultural boxes before we get to know them as individuals. They made the case that there are individual differences, but not cultural difference. Some in the class strongly objected to the whole concept of culture. These students had a point. Yes, we must get to know people as individuals without oversimplistic ideas about them. Besides, there is enormous variability within each culture.

But culture matters. Neighbors influence neighbors. Families profoundly shape their children. Cultural values significantly influence
teaching and learning. Effective teachers acknowledge individual differences within cultural contexts and realize that all human beings have
much in common no matter their personality or culture. We are all the
same yet different.

It seems like common sense, so it's a bit surprising when I observe
teachers ignoring culture. I asked one of my Canadian friends teaching
Bible knowledge classes in a Nigerian government secondary school
how he was adapting his teaching style to Nigeria. He answered, "I
don't adapt to culture; I just teach the Bible and let the chips fall
where they may." For him teaching the Bible in a rural Nigerian school
was no different from teaching in a Canadian classroom. Culture
didn't matter. His students may have done well on the government
Bible knowledge exam, but I doubt if his teaching made much impact
on their daily lives. Culturally blind teaching can occur when Guatemalans teach in India, Koreans teach in Zambia, or Australians
teach in Ecuador.

An African friend told of an American professor who came to his
school to teach pastoral theology. The professor announced that he
would begin the class with an icebreaker. This confused the students,
who had little experience with ice and had no idea why they needed
an icebreaker. Later in the course, he taught that pastors should
comfort a person who had just lost a loved one. He said that those
going through deep sorrow need to be alone, and that maybe one
person at a time should visit the bereaved person for just a few
minutes. The African students were shocked. They all knew that when
a person died, the whole community felt obligated to surround the
grieving person and stay for days. The American professor failed to
understand he came from an individualistic culture and his principles
of pastoral theology reflected his cultural values. He didn't understand
how pastoral theology practices might be radically different in a
collectivistic culture.

Cultural values influence every aspect of teaching and learning, yet we are seldom aware of them. A famous fable illustrates the point. Two young fish are swimming along, and they happen to meet an older fish swimming the other way. The older fish says, "Good morning, boys, how's the water?" The two young fish swim on for a bit, and then one of them eventually looks over at the other and asks, "What is water?" An old Chinese proverb says, "If you want to know about water, don't ask the fish."

Edward T. Hall likens culture to an invisible jet stream that influences weather around the world.[1] The jet stream controls the wind, rain, snow, warmth, and cold over a whole continent, yet it is imperceptible to our eyes. In the same way hidden cultural currents shape our assumptions about the time and place of teaching, instructional methods and objectives, assumptions about the roles of teacher and student, educational evaluation, and much more. In spite of globalization, implicit cultural paradigms continue to exert a powerful influence on teaching.

Each individual is both distinct from and alike to all other humans. If each of us were totally unique in every way, crosscultural teaching would be impossible. But if we're all the same, why bother with a book that helps us teach people different from ourselves? All human beings are created in the image of God and have a common human nature. Yet our families and communities promote different cultural values. At the same time each individual has a distinct personality. Let's look at the delightful complexity of human beings.

One way to understand the complexity of human beings is to take into account what is the same in all people and where we differ. In my crosscultural classes I've used a segmented triangle to illustrate similarities and differences.[2] The larger base of the triangle makes the point that fundamentally we are all created in the image of God and have a

---

[1] Edward T. Hall, *Beyond Culture* (Garden City, NY: Anchor Books, 1997), 12.
[2] I first discovered the triangle describing human beings in Geert Hofstede, Gert Jan Hofstede, and Michael Minkov, *Cultures and Organizations: Software of the Mind*, 3rd ed. (Chicago: McGraw-Hill, 2010), 6.

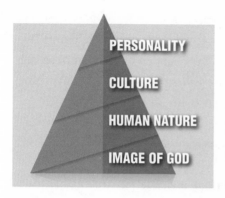

Figure 4.1. Similarities and differences among humans

common human nature. But we are all enfolded into cultural communities where we have commonalities as well as differences. Finally, each person has a unique personality (see fig. 4.1).

IMAGE OF GOD

As astounding as it may seem to the secular world, the Bible teaches that in the depth of our being, all of us are made by God in his image (Gen 1:27). Because all humans bear God's likeness, each person has unimaginable worth and dignity. C. S. Lewis says,

> It is a serious thing to live in a society of possible gods and goddesses, to remember that the dullest and most uninteresting person you talk to may one day be a creature, if you saw it now, you would be strongly tempted to worship, or else a horror and a corruption such as you now meet, if at all, only in a nightmare. . . . There are no ordinary people. You have never talked to a mere mortal.[3]

Lewis makes the point that all human beings are growing toward either "immortal horrors or everlasting splendours."[4] Every individual is growing in one of two directions—either growing more and more into the image of God or moving away from his splendor. The ultimate aim of education is to foster the development of students so that more and more they become all that God created them to become.

No mere mortals! We need to look at people from God's perspective. People are important regardless of how smart, wealthy, or athletic they are. Nations come and go, but people live forever. From God's perspective, there are no insignificant students. Everyone, from every culture, is created in the image of God. This is the capstone concept for *why* we teach, *what* we teach, *how* we teach, and *who* we teach.

---

[3]C. S. Lewis, *The Weight of Glory* (New York: Collier Books, 1975), 19.
[4]Lewis, *Weight of Glory*, 20.

HUMAN NATURE

In spite of significant cultural and personality differences, we are fundamentally alike. Because our similarities are greater than our differences, we can be encouraged at the prospect of learning how to teach and be taught in any culture. We all have similar physical, social, intellectual, and spiritual needs. Even though we may have different physical features and cultural backgrounds, most people have eyes, ears, vocal cords, a sense of touch and taste; blood types and internal organs can be interchanged with any other human being. Our common basic needs, developmental processes, and brain structures make communication possible. We can teach well crossculturally because of our common humanity.

CULTURE

Of course, we make a serious mistake if we conclude that since we are all human, culture doesn't matter. The critical role of culture challenges us to be humble lifelong learners, while our common humanity gives us optimism.

As teachers we face the danger of either putting too much emphasis on culture or simply ignoring it. By overemphasizing the role of culture we can become discouraged by the complex, subtle differences and then feel it is hopeless to attempt to teach across cultures. Ignoring cultural differences leads to embarrassing misunderstandings and ineffective teaching.

In a shrinking world, teachers and students travel from all around the world to teach and study. Americans study in Singapore, Chinese in Scotland, Ghanaians in Kenya, and Malaysians in Canada. I recently taught a graduate course in Addis Ababa, Ethiopia, and in Seoul, Korea. In both Ethiopia and Korea, I met expatriate teachers from dozens of countries around the world. At universities where I've taught, I've been delighted to have fellow professors from China, Korea, Burkina Faso, Germany, Australia, and more. My classes at Trinity Evangelical Divinity School are delightfully filled with students from around the world. Since culture continues to be a powerful influence, it is more important than ever for teachers to understand crosscultural education paradigms. Culture matters.

The quandary of culture's influence is that most of it is below the level of our awareness. Anthropologist Edward T. Hall also wrote that "culture hides more than it reveals, and strangely enough what it hides, it hides most effectively from its own participants."[5] The hiddenness of culture presents a challenge to crosscultural teachers. Most of the time both teachers and students have pictures in their minds about proper ways to teach and learn, but their mental pictures may be very different.

INDIVIDUAL PERSONALITY

One of the dangers of overemphasizing culture is that we might stereotype people, assuming that because a person comes from a certain culture they are like everyone else in that culture. The peak of the pyramid depicts personality differences. Yes, every human is created in the image of God and has much in common with every other human being. We may be similar culturally. Yet every person is unique. Those of us who teach across cultures can gain important insights from cultural values, but we need to be aware of individual distinctions as well.

In my first evening of teaching in Ethiopia I was struck by how unique each student was. Some were inquisitive and challenged me as the professor; others didn't say anything unless I called on them. Some were shy, others outgoing. One woman illustrated her point with abstract logic, another young man rambled on with vigorous hand gestures. Some students gave practical applications while others gave deep philosophical insights. I suspect that most personality types were present in the class. As the class progressed, I was excited to learn more and more about each student. Even in the same culture these students demonstrated educational differences, gender differences, personality differences, and differences in work experiences.

My experiences in crosscultural teaching were helpful in providing a general framework for understanding the culture of Ethiopian students.

---

[5]Edward T. Hall, *The Silent Language* (Greenwich, CT: Fawcett, 1959), 39.

I appreciated their polite greetings and wasn't surprised when few of the students arrived on time. Although caught off guard, I wasn't offended when students insisted on carrying my briefcase. Cultural similarities among the students were obvious, but individual differences were equally important. As the class proceeded, I learned to use their individual differences to help me teach. I learned who to call on first, who needed encouragement to speak, and who might share from their experience. I also tried to apply the concepts of my teaching to the specific ministry situations of individual students.

AVOIDING STEREOTYPES

While appreciating cultural differences is critical for the crosscultural teacher, it isn't wise to make simplistic assumptions about individuals merely because they come from a certain culture. Culture has a powerful influence, yet each individual is unique and is continually changing. Overgeneralizing can be as unhelpful as ignoring cultural differences.

Another caution is that culture itself is dynamic, and cultural values change. Rural farmers migrate to megacities; children go to school rather than learning from the hands-on teaching of their grandparents. Schooling, urbanization, and travel promote flexibility in cultural values. Second-generation children of immigrants live in a world different from their parents. Government policies may also have a strong influence, such as the one-child-policy in China. Dynamic changes profoundly influence expectations about education.

My mom and dad were both born in Ohio, both attended Ohio State University, and both sang in the church choir. They both came to have a deep commitment to be followers of Jesus Christ and had a lifelong happy marriage. But in other ways they were as different as night and day.

Similar subcultures have common cultural values. In the United States, Amish, African American, Asian American, and Latino communities tend to form subcultures. Similar subcultures exist in every country. When professors from Trinity International University in Deerfield, forty miles north of Chicago, teach evening classes in an extension campus on the south side of Chicago, they experience significant cultural differences that influence their teaching. When highly educated urban Bolivians make a presentation in an isolated rural village, they are teaching in a subculture.

Teachers and students react differently in different contexts. A student may treat the teacher with respect in the classroom, but then tease the teacher at a school party. This might be seen as disrespectable behavior in some cultures.

Understanding cultural perspectives is useful for crosscultural teaching because these give us cues for responding to puzzling situations. But because of cultural complexity, these insights may not predict how a person will behave. For example, it isn't helpful for me to look at a Latino and predict that this person will have a high tolerance for ambiguity. Many Latinos do, but many do not. Still, when I see a Latino-designed conference with a completely flexible timetable, I'm not surprised. I understand that the ability to tolerate ambiguity is a common trait. So an understanding of culture is useful for *describing* and analyzing a situation, but not as useful for *prescribing* how it should be.

THE ADAPTABLE TEACHER

Pedagogical flexibility isn't easy, but it's rewarding. Becoming fluent in more than one teaching style is like learning to be fluent in more than one language. Nobody gets it right the first time or even the second or third time, but that's all right. Perhaps the key to successful crosscultural teaching is the ability to be curious and flexible toward other cultures.

ASKING GREAT QUESTIONS

By Jose Luis Baldera from the Dominican Republic, teaching in El Salvador

We Dominicans have the peculiarity of all talking at the same time in a loud tone as if we are shouting or arguing. We use a lot of slang (*pa'qué* instead of *para qué*). We don't pronounce our *s*'s either (e.g., *Tabamo* instead of saying *estabamos*).

On top of this, the velocity and idioms we use can result in the conclusion that to understand a Dominican, you have to study extraterrestrial languages.

With this in mind, I found that the Salvadorans I was teaching didn't understand half of what I was saying, and they usually just laughed. My tone of voice was so strong that people would turn their heads and think something was wrong.

I assumed that the Salvadorans would interrupt me to give their opinion, as we do. I talked nonstop and felt I had to keep talking. With time, I realized I needed to pause and give others the opportunity to ask questions or make comments.

I needed to learn how to encourage interaction and discussion without talking so much myself. How could I create space for others to participate? How could I speak without sounding intimidating or frightening?

I found the answers in a course titled "Building Relationships." I learned what it means to have empathy. I learned that teaching isn't about telling everything I know, but about listening and understanding what the students know. I was captured by the idea of open questions. Still, it's easier to understand a concept than to put it into practice.

Sometimes my open questions only resulted in lost expressions on my students' faces. I would modify the question, but even then they kept looking at me like a stranger. I would simplify the questions and get some kind of answer, but not to what I was asking. I would sigh and begin again, tempted to ask a question that contained the answer. With calmness and careful thought, I reformulated the question and finally received interaction.

With time, my tone of voice has become softer, and I speak more slowly. I practice with my children, asking good questions that will help them think. I'm finding that great questions are the secret to helpful reflection and interaction.

TEACHING AND CONTEXT

I have become all things to all people
so that by all possible means I might save some.

1 CORINTHIANS 9:22

To come out of one's house means learning.

KIKUYU PROVERB

TEACHERS TEACH IN TWO WAYS—by what they say and by what they don't say. In much of the world, facial expressions and tone of voice communicate even more than words. Once during a small doctoral seminar, I was leaning back in my chair with my hands folded behind my head. I'm sure I was expounding on a most important idea when a student from Ghana interrupted and wanted to know why I was angry with him. I sat up straight and apologetically assured him that I was in no way angry with him. He then demanded to know why I had my hands on my head. I told him it was because I was enjoying the class and felt relaxed. From this student's experience, putting my hands on my head was a sign of anger, and my nonverbal communication unintentionally spoke more than my precise words. We teachers always communicate a lot more and a lot less than we think we do.

Some of the most prestigious professors in my culture read their lectures in a monotone voice. Their words are so important that they don't want to trivialize the information with shouting or hand motions. Too much emotion might demonstrate a lack of intellectual rigor. For these teachers, ideas communicate everything and shouldn't be degraded by distracting nonverbal communication. But I've lived much of my life with teachers from a different perspective. Much of what they communicate is through the context: classroom arrangement, the teacher's dress, tone of voice, emotions, and body movement. From the perspective of low-context lecturers, these high-context teachers who walk around the classroom waving their arms and shouting may seem poorly organized because the main point is not clearly outlined. In high-context cultures, students themselves are expected to discover a principle behind the many stories.

During one of my trips to Cape Town, South Africa, I preached to a staid, formal Afrikaans congregation. One of my Dutch friends advised me ahead of time on how to preach. I climbed up to a high pulpit and looked down on quiet, thoughtful people with their hands in their laps. I tried to be as formal as possible, preaching a well-organized sermon with subpoints of the main topic. I tried to match my teaching style with the cultural expectations of the congregation where words were the primary means of communication.

On that same trip I was invited to preach in a large black African Zionist church in Durban, South Africa. I was the second preacher of the evening, and the first one greatly intimidated me. There was no way I could preach like him! He moved around the platform telling story after story, sometimes shouting and sometimes whispering. He'd often stop to take a drink of water and wipe the sweat from his forehead. I realized right away that I would be a dull preacher, but I tried my best. At times I raised my voice and even shouted occasionally while walking around the platform. I felt more like an actor than a preacher, realizing that no matter how hard I tried I couldn't keep up with the real preacher. Even though I was a second-rate preacher, several in the congregation gave me a loud *amen* and one or two raised their hands.

High-context preaching is not inherently better or worse than low-context preaching. The task of the preacher is to adapt as much as possible to the expectations of the congregation. I tried to be flexible in my preaching, focusing on words in the low-context congregation and trying to connect with the high-context congregation through active participation.

PERSONALITY DIFFERENCES

Personality also influences how much people are aware of their context. My parents are a good example of two people from the same culture with significant personality differences.

Mom was high-context. She was constantly aware of people—their facial expressions, their body language, their feelings. She never forgot the people she'd met and remembered almost everything about past conversations—their names, their children, and even what they were wearing. When I was a teenager, she could read my nonverbal clues and facial expressions, which often got me into trouble. Mom was very attuned to her context.

My dad was a low-context research chemist who earned a hundred patents in his lifetime. At home in the evening he would read the newspaper, work on a crossword puzzle, and design a lab experiment for the next day—all at the same time. I once asked him about the little pencil squiggles in the margin of the newspaper. He nonchalantly replied that he was designing a new molecule that might help to glue heat shield tiles to the space shuttle. He lived in the world of abstract ideas. But my dad couldn't remember names and often forgot about past events. I once observed him teaching a high school Sunday school class. He didn't remember the names of the kids in his class, so he called every boy "George" and every girl "Suzie." In a rather demanding voice he would ask. "George, what is the main emphasis of 1 Corinthians 13?" The kid would respond, "My name isn't George!" Dad said, "No problem, what is the main point of 1 Corinthians 13?" The girls objected to being called Suzie, but Dad didn't seem to notice. He just wanted to know if they had the right answer. My dad primarily lived in the world of ideas and didn't pay as much attention to the context around him.

Mom was sensitive to peoples' feelings; Dad, not as much. I remember a time at a Wednesday night prayer meeting when the preacher in our rural Methodist church made a mistake in the use of a Greek word.

My dad corrected him—right in the middle of the sermon. On the way home, my mom was incredulous. "Edwin, do you know how much you embarrassed the preacher tonight? In front of the whole congregation too! How could you do such a thing?" Dad merely replied, "I was right, wasn't I?"

Dad lived in the world of ideas while Mom was very aware of the surrounding context—the people, sights, sounds, smells. Both were godly, gifted people, but they were very different in their response to the context around them. Though dad was less aware of the context around him, he was aware of important ideas, which led to dozens of astounding practical inventions. Words were his primary method of communication. All people are to some extent aware of their context and also are able to think abstractly, but preferences toward one or the other tend to differ. Maybe a better way of describing the difference is to identify my mom as more *context aware* and my dad as more *idea aware*.

Interestingly, children loved my dad, and he enjoyed children. At a church picnic, Dad would rather go on an "elephant hunt" with the children than sit around, small-talking with adults. When neighborhood children came to our house, they often asked if "Jimmy's dad could come out and play."

ARISTOTLE OR CONFUCIUS?

While early Greek philosophy concerned itself with abstract syllogisms and logical geometric proofs, traditional Eastern educational philosophy emphasized the applied: harmonious society, right posture, right breathing, and controlled desires.

University of Michigan professor Richard E. Nisbett was challenged by one of his Chinese students who commented, "You know, the difference between you and me is that I think the world is a circle and you think it's a line."[1] Nisbett was pushed to rethink his assumptions about the universality of how people think. Together with his

---

[1]Richard E. Nisbett, *The Geography of Thought: How Asians and Westerners Think Differently . . . and Why* (New York: Free Press, 2003), xiii.

Asian students, he conducted research at Beijing University, Kyoto University, Seoul National University, and the Chinese Institute of Psychology. Nisbett reported his findings in the book *The Geography of Thought: How Asians and Westerners Think Differently . . . and Why.* Many of my students from Africa and Latin America have observed that they identified more with Asian thinking than Western philosophy.

Nisbett begins, "More than a billion people in the world today claim intellectual inheritance from ancient Greece. More than two billion are the heirs of ancient Chinese traditions of thought."[2] Aristotle taught individual freedom, creativity, and happiness. He valued curiosity and categorized objects in nature. The word *school* comes from the Greek meaning "leisure" or the freedom to indulge in debate.[3] In contrast, Confucius taught self-control, obedience to authority, and the importance of social harmony. Debate might disrupt harmony and authority. Greek thinking emphasized categorization based on abstract concepts. According to Nisbett, Taoism, Confucianism, and Buddhism "emphasized harmony and largely discouraged abstract speculation."[4] He writes, "The concern with abstraction characteristic of ancient Greek philosophy has no counterpart in Chinese philosophy. Chinese philosophers quite explicitly favored the most concrete sense impressions in understanding the world."[5]

Asian thinking tended to see objects in their context, while Western thinking dichotomized and categorized objects independent of their context. One interesting experiment compared students from the University of Michigan and Kyoto University. Both sets of students were shown pictures of underwater scenes. Participants were asked to describe what they saw. Japanese students tended to describe the environment—the water, rocks, bubbles, plants, and the fish. American students were more likely to zero in on individual fish, ignoring the context. The researcher Taka Masuda suggested that "Asians view the world through

---

[2]Nisbett, *Geography of Thought*, 1.
[3]Nisbett, *Geography of Thought*, 4.
[4]Nisbett, *Geography of Thought*, 12.
[5]Nisbett, *Geography of Thought*, 17.

a wide-angle lens, whereas Westerners have tunnel vision."[6] While it is important to avoid stereotyping individuals, the insights from *The Geography of Thought* can be helpful when we observe differences.

TEACHING AND CONTEXT

There are many ways to categorize cultural values, but for me the most overarching cultural value is the extent to which people are aware of their context. Nisbett refers to Edward T. Hall's concept of high- and low-context cultures as an aspect of communication.[7] Since the primary role of teachers is to communicate effectively, Hall's studies are important for the crosscultural teacher. In typical high-context cultures, people live in close-knit communities, and even subtle, nonverbal body language is completely understood by family and neighbors. In these high-context communities, folks intuitively sense what others are thinking. Hall observes that for most of our history

> our forefathers knew the significance of every act of all the individuals around them. . . . Living today in a rapidly changing, ever-shrinking world, it is hard for most of us to conceive what it would be like to grow up and live in a world that did not change, and where there were few strangers because one always saw and dealt with the same people. . . . People knew what was coming next before you did something or even that you were going to do it. "Jake is going to get a new horse." "Yup. He always fattens up the old one before he trades. Too cheap to feed 'em the rest of the time."[8]

Context alone communicates significant amounts of data for those living in traditional small towns and villages. In the local restaurant, a man merely clears his throat and the waitress knows he wants more coffee. When Grandma Smith walks in the door, the cook begins to fry two strips of bacon and a couple of pancakes. The communication is in the context, not in the verbal code.

Hall contends that most people in the world live in high-context cultures where communication is implicit and words aren't as needed

---

[6]Taka Masuda, quoted in Nisbett, *Geography of Thought*, 89.
[7]Nisbett, *Geography of Thought*, 83.
[8]Edward T. Hall, *Beyond Culture* (Garden City, NY: Anchor Books, 1997), 41.

to convey meaning. *What* is said doesn't communicate as much as *who* said it, *where* it was said, and *how* it was said.

On the other hand, in low-context cultures words themselves are the primary mode of communication. The context doesn't communicate as much. This is because communication in low-context cultures takes place between people who have had little previous interaction. Since they have not learned the nonverbal cues, communication needs to be explicit. Written words carry almost no contextual meaning, and this can lead to misunderstanding.

Emails, for example, often come across in a cold way. During a trip to Niger, I was approached by a Nigerien pastor who was confused by a letter he received from a pastor in the United States. What the American pastor wrote was clear enough, but the Nigerien pastor was sure that what *wasn't* said, or what was written between the lines, was the real message. The low-context words on paper were difficult for a high-context pastor to comprehend.

Subtle, nonverbal body language is often missing from social media and technology where people don't have the contextual cues of tone of voice or facial expression. Some folks have suggested there should be a sarcasm font to help people who don't realize that something is being said sarcastically. It's interesting that emoji are actually an attempt to reintroduce facial expressions and emotions to a low-context medium.[9]

There are strengths in both high- and low-context communication. In a globalizing world where few people know those with whom they interact, low-context communication is absolutely necessary. One reason my dad tended toward the low end of the context spectrum was because his mind was in a different place. He was thinking of ideas, abstractions, and theories. He was always asking himself *why* things happened the way they did. My mom was more practical and concrete in her thinking. She wasn't as interested in why something worked, she just wanted to make it work.

Of course no culture or individual is totally high or low context; most are somewhere toward the middle. Some people straddle both

---

[9]This idea about emojis was pointed out to me by my editor, Al Hsu.

ways of thinking. The setting is also significant. Students may be more low context in the classroom and more high context while cheering for their sports team.

A common problem with teachers from low-context countries is that they pay more attention to the subject matter than to the students. And a common problem with high-context students is that they pay more attention to the professor than to the subject matter.[10]

Those who teach across cultures need to be aware that in much of the world, the very idea of a schoolroom is countercultural. Schooling by its nature is low context, as reading and writing are the primary means of conveying information. In earlier times children learned about farming while observing their fathers on the farm and learned about cooking by helping their mothers cook. Traditional education was high context, but the modern schoolroom is isolated from the context.

Schooling teaches students to sit still and pay attention to the teacher, who communicates primarily with words. The first Sunday we arrived in Nigeria, I sat in the back of a Sunday school class that met in the waiting room of Kano Eye Hospital. The room was packed with children, yet more and more kept coming, scrunching together more tightly on the hospital benches. Older girls carried crying babies on their backs, while boys wandered in and out talking with each other. Hardly anyone paid attention to the teacher. Old men wandered up and down the isles swatting misbehaving children with long, pliable sticks. Nigerian church leaders saw me as the expert in Christian education and asked for advice on how to improve Sunday school. I had two degrees in Christian education, but nothing I learned in America seemed to apply to this context. I was stymied. Almost in despair, I realized that my training assumed a culture of specific age groups, small classrooms, detailed curriculum, and life-related applications. My real education began in Nigeria when the assumptions of my old paradigm were shattered. I then began to see the possibilities of the more integrated pilgrim paradigm.

---

[10]Hall, *Beyond Culture*, 88.

BECOMING BILINGUAL IN SPANISH

By David Delgado from Costa Rica, teaching in Panama

Students' faces displayed question marks. For a moment, no one said anything, but the gestures said it all. The sweat on my hands and my mental battle told me something wasn't right, but I couldn't understand what it was. The presentation was adequate. The materials and resources were suitable, and the concepts had been explained well.

But why were the students looking that way? What did I do? Could it be that I had said something heretical and was about to be thrown to the bonfire? Suddenly a hand went up and saved my day. "Excuse me, professor, what does that word mean that you just used?" Now everything made sense. It wasn't what I had said but the word I used to say it.

I explained the meaning of the word, and now everything returned to normal. I discreetly wiped the sweat off my hands.

Even though we speak Spanish in almost all of Latin America, it seems that our ancestors did not agree on a unified language. Instead, each country decided to decorate it in the way they thought best, separating it from the rest. I believe that teaching in another culture, even if the language is the same, is a challenge. With their own expressions, indigenous exclamations, regional sayings, and different meanings, speaking and writing become both a challenge and valuable opportunity.

I've taken advantage of this opportunity to soak myself in the language of the people. I've needed to go to markets and to parks on public busses and converse with as many people as possible to better understand the right style of Spanish in another culture. This has helped me to overcome teaching barriers. Although it is a continuous learning process, it's certainly not boring, and I have become "bilingual in Spanish." Though I'm still learning, I am benefiting from the heritage of my ancestors.

6

TEACHING AND CULTURAL VALUES

Culture hides more than it reveals, and strangely enough what it hides, it hides most effectively from its own participants.

Edward T. Hall

I WAS A BIT WORRIED as I stepped off the plane. I was about to spend a week with twenty experiential education professors from seventeen countries in Latin America. I didn't know the schedule or how often I was to speak. I wasn't even sure of the topic. I assumed, though, that I could discover what was expected of me on the ride from the airport to the conference center. Lisa, the organizer, was a good friend and former student, but she didn't ease my uncertainty. She told me I could do whatever I wanted and that the only scheduled items were meals. Apparently, I was the only one on the week-long program from 8 a.m. to 10 p.m. every day! I kept questioning her all the way to the conference center: "Do you want me to talk about leadership, about teaching, about curriculum, about evaluation, about human development?" Lisa replied, "Do whatever you wish." I was a bit frustrated. To be fair, she had previously emailed me detailed profiles for each of the participants, so I had a pretty good sense of who they were. She trusted me to come prepared with a variety of modules that I could adapt to this setting. Lisa helped me understand the context of my teaching, but not the content, the timing, or objectives. I wondered if she was testing me.

My mistake was that I assumed the old educational paradigm of a low tolerance for ambiguity. I expected a conference with clear objectives, a timetable for every hour or so, and topics for each session. I assumed the participants expected PowerPoint presentations with handouts for each session. How could I prepare presentations and handouts if I didn't know what they wanted me to teach? None of the Latino professors seemed perturbed that there was no seminar topic, handouts, or a timetable.

When I arrived at the conference center, I asked if I could meet with the professors after dinner. Since they were most at ease in Spanish, I worked through a translator the whole week. (I wished I'd paid more attention to my Spanish studies in college.) After dinner, we sat outside in a circle and introduced ourselves, giving important details about various aspects of our lives. This continued for a couple of hours. I then asked them what they wanted to think about during the week and what concerns they had as professors. Each person gave suggestions, and I soon had general teaching ideas for the whole week. We continued our discussion, talking and listening, until late into the evening. Then I went to my room and prepared the teaching for the next day. This happened all week. I didn't specifically know what we would be discussing the second day until we finished the first day. Yet the week was rich with interaction and mutual learning.

This story is an example of how cultural paradigms influence expectations in education. It's true that we live in a globalizing world where just about every culture borrows from every other culture, and educational expectations are becoming more and more intertwined. Yet this story illustrates differences in tolerance for ambiguity and how these impact teaching.

TEACHING AND AMBIGUITY

Most of us live in an unpredictable world where the future is always uncertain. Some cultures don't worry much about uncertainty, and others do everything possible to mitigate it. Those who tolerate ambiguity may assume there is little they can do to control the future. "Que será será, / Whatever will be, will be." On the other hand, people with a low tolerance for ambiguity try to control the future with long-range planning, thick policy manuals, detailed to-do lists, and tightly scheduled appointments. Cultural values about ambiguity and predictability significantly influence crosscultural teaching.

Those from my German background usually prefer teaching to be predictable with clear objectives and prepared lessons. Around the world, formal educational systems by nature seek to avoid ambiguity, as is seen in "teaching for the test" and detailed lesson plans. On the other hand, people outside of the formal schooling system might have a higher tolerance for ambiguity. For them life is unpredictable, so it's no surprise that teaching and learning are serendipitous as well.

The planning strategy for the conference I described was "Let's get together with some interesting people in a comfortable setting and see what happens." And great things happened!

Tensions may surface when global conferences are scheduled by leaders who have a low tolerance for ambiguity with many participants who have a high tolerance for ambiguity. These participants might enjoy "going with the flow" and "as the Spirit leads" rather than sticking to rigid timetables. Yet the logistics of bringing hundreds of people together for a limited amount of time can be extremely challenging and require some kind of time orientation. While some of my Latin American friends were appreciative of the Cape Town 2010 Lausanne congress, they were frustrated by the precise time limitations on the speakers. They mentioned a massive clock in the back of the auditorium that counted down the seconds left for the speaker, and felt this constrained the leading of the Holy Spirit. Yet most of the speakers would not have had an opportunity to make their presentations if the conference had not been designed by time-oriented planners. It would be interesting to attempt to plan a global consultation where planners from both high- and low-ambiguity perspectives could respectfully work from each other's viewpoints.

Teachers and students from cultures with a low tolerance for ambiguity prefer detailed classroom manuals, measurable objectives, meticulous lesson plans, written lectures, and tightly guided discussion. Insecure teachers may be afraid that students will ask questions they don't know the answer for. Or they are concerned about not having enough content to fill the whole hour. So the insecure teacher who is uncomfortable with uncertainty will write out a lecture packed with lots of information illustrated with PowerPoint slides and leave little time for class discussion.

There is often a correlation between a high tolerance for ambiguity and high-context cultures. High-context people tolerate ambiguity because events going on around them are more important than the disruption of a low-context clock. Teachers from a high-context culture are not as concerned about planning or predictable objectives. They would say, "How can one plan when the context is continually changing? Ambiguity is a fact of life, so live with it!" Those of us from low-context cultures feel ill at ease when we aren't sure where we are headed or what will happen next. We fear ambiguity.

School teachers in the United States are compelled to avoid ambiguity by being required to accomplish predetermined learning outcomes each day. Lesson plans must be prepared well in advance and approved by the supervisor. School districts, principals, and individual teachers are evaluated according to student scores on standardized tests. The context of the student's home and community environment is almost irrelevant to the context-independent exams. The American school system has become the epitome of avoiding uncertainty. It's difficult for modern public school teachers to imagine a school without precise learning objectives, specific teaching time, or formal evaluation. The emphasis on testing with No Child Left Behind and a national Common Core Curriculum allows little room for the ambiguity of tangential discussions or creative thinking. In spite of this straightjacket educational system that avoids ambiguity, many teachers have figured out how to connect with their students and relate knowledge to the context.

Students in Finland consistently score at or near the top on international tests of student achievement. Yet when teachers from Finland begin to teach in the United States, they often feel stifled by the rigidity of American schools. One Finnish teacher in the United States describes her teaching as "a rote job where she follows a curriculum she didn't develop herself, keeps a principal-dictated schedule, and sits in meetings where details aren't debated." She continues, "I feel rushed, nothing gets done properly; there is very little joy, and no time for reflection or creative thinking."[1]

Modern education around the world has also moved away from a high tolerance for ambiguity. Traditional education in most of the world was deeply embedded in the context. Boys learned how to farm by observing and imitating their fathers, and girls absorbed the duties of their mother by watching, mimicking, and receiving immediate feedback. Teachable moments throughout the day provided meaningful, though ambiguous, education. Today, the majority of formal schooling systems throughout the world aim for uniform, predictable results.

In Asia, Africa, Latin America, and Europe, the emphasis on passing noncontext-related exams can inhibit meaningful learning. Ambiguity is anathema. After-school cram classes are common in much of Asia to prepare for "examination hell." An article in the *BBC News* magazine reports that cheating is common among wealthy students in Uttar Pradesh, India, who can afford to purchase tests ahead of time.[2] Thus poor students feel they should be allowed to cheat as well. One university student claimed, "Cheating is our democratic right!" and another, "Cheating is our birthright."

Globally, formal education is becoming more and more divorced from the real world of the learner and is often just a means for passing exams in order to get into the best schools, in order to earn high salaries. Learning for the joy of learning or for the sake of an enriched life is diminished when systems can't tolerate ambiguity.

Again, educational flexibility is the key to effective crosscultural teaching. Teachers with a low tolerance for ambiguity need to be ready to adapt to ambiguous educational settings. Teachers who appreciate flexible teaching can adapt to a more rigid schedule. Understanding this cultural difference is another big step toward being effective.

---

[1]Timothy D. Walker, "When Finnish Teachers Work in America's Public Schools," *The Atlantic*, November 28, 2016, www.theatlantic.com/education/archive/2016/11/when-finnish-teachers-work-in-americas-public-schools/508685.

[2]Craig Jeffrey, "Students Who Feel They Have the Right to Cheat," BBC News, November 9, 2014, www.bbc.com/news/magazine-29950843.

Teaching and Power Distance

When Asian students at Trinity come to class, they often give me a slight bow and formally say, "Good morning, Dr. Plueddemann." They are astounded when American students walk into class with a casual "Hi Jim." One undergrad student even greeted me with "Hi dude." In one doctoral seminar, I nonchalantly leaned back in my chair and put my stocking feet on the table (and one sock had a hole). Observing the surprise on the faces of my international students, I quickly put my feet on the floor and sat up straight.

Why is it that many of my American students speak up in class without being called on, while some international students seldom speak unless I call on them? In my classes, a couple of students are quick to challenge each other and even disagree with me, the professor. I very much enjoy such debates. Most students from other cultures (and there are notable exceptions) prefer harmony in class and would never think of challenging the professor.

An understanding of power distance in education is another essential focus for the crosscultural teacher. Geert Hofstede defines power distance as "the extent to which the less powerful members of institutions and organizations within a country expect and accept that power is distributed unequally."[3] In high-power-distance cultures, both the teacher and the students assume that the teacher has more authority, requiring respect and status symbols. Students don't challenge their teachers. They carry their teachers' briefcases, greet them formally, and assume they will wear formal clothes. High-power-distance students feel honored to have a high-status teacher who exhibits symbols of prestige.

Teachers in low-power-distance cultures delight in heated class discussion. They are not surprised when students challenge the teacher's authority, suggest a modified assignment, or question their grade. Teachers avoid status symbols such as wearing a suit and tie while teaching. Both the teacher and the students assume there is little power

---

[3]Geert Hofstede, Gert Jan Hofstede, and Michael Minkov, *Cultures and Organizations: Software of the Mind*, 3rd ed. (Chicago: McGraw-Hill, 2010), 46.

distance between them. Being a buddy to the professor, calling them by their first name, and feeling free to phone the professor at home is common in low-power-distance educational settings.

I asked an academically gifted Asian student why he never asked a question in class. He explained to me the importance of *saving face*. "If the student asks a question, it means either that the student isn't intelligent or that the professor isn't very good at explaining the subject matter. Either way the student or the teacher loses face." For a student to raise a hand in the middle of a lecture from a high-power-distance professor would be an insult to the professor. For the professor to ignore the student in a low-power-distance culture would be taken as an insult to the student.

A girl in Liberia came home from school one day and said she had learned that spiders have six legs. Her Australian friend corrected her by pointing out that spiders have eight legs. They solved the question by finding a spider and counting the legs. The next day the girl took the spider to school and announced to the teacher and the class that spiders have eight legs, not six legs. Her teacher promptly punished her by whacking her on the hand with a stick. The number of legs on the spider was insignificant compared to making the teacher lose face.

When I was preparing to preach in Korean churches, my host took me to a barber for a haircut and then bought me a couple of dignified neckties. Should I have been offended? My gracious host wasn't insulting me. He was helping me to overcome my natural low-power-distance informality in order to gain credibility in Korean churches.

The skill of teaching across cultures requires that we recognize the perspectives of the other culture and adapt as much as possible. I still have much to learn and need to be more formal when teaching high-power-distance students. In a classroom with students from both perspectives I try to help each group understand the other. I was delighted one day when a Korean student good-humoredly gave me a phony bow and said, "Hi, Dr. Jim," while an American student playfully bowed deeply and addressed me as "The Most Rev. Dr. Professor Plueddemann." Our multicultural classes become living laboratories for understanding, appreciating, and even enjoying cultural differences in education.

TEACHING IN INDIVIDUALISTIC OR COLLECTIVISTIC CULTURES

I often begin class by summarizing an exceptional paper from one of the students. I do this to affirm the student and give the rest of the class a model of what I'm looking for in a paper. I realized that I'd made a mistake when I acknowledged the strong points of a paper by a Malaysian student. He looked embarrassed, and I could sense that I had offended him. After class he graciously approached me and quoted a proverb: "The nail that sticks up is the one that gets pounded." It was awkward for him to be singled out from the rest of the class. A similar Ecuadorian proverb says, "The longest blade of grass is the first to be cut down." In collectivistic cultures, praising the group is more appropriate than honoring an individual.

My doctoral mentor, Ted Ward, visited us in Nigeria. One evening he asked me to take him to a theological college near Jos in order to gather some data on cognitive style and culture. After handing out the test sheets in the classroom, he clearly warned, "This test measures the ways *individuals* think. There is no right or wrong answer, but don't cheat." As soon as he said "Begin" all the students started to talk to each other and work on each other's papers. Ted stopped them immediately. I could sense he was worried that after coming all the way to Nigeria his data would be corrupted and worthless. He sternly warned them again, "Don't cheat!" As soon as he said "Go" the students again began to work on each other's papers. Exasperated, Ted asked, "What is going on? Why are you cheating?" A seminary student in the back of the room announced, "Sir, for us to cheat is to withhold information from a brother who needs it."

Possibly the most researched cultural value is the contrast between cultures that are individualistic and those that are collectivistic. Cultures that value individualism strive for personal achievement, independence, self-esteem, freedom of choice, and personal responsibility. Collectivistic cultures value harmony, family honor, and communal success.

In one of my classes I gave students a sheet of paper with the words "I am" and a long blank space. This was repeated ten times down the page. I asked students to describe themselves by giving ten words or phrases to tell who they are. While there was some overlap, non-Western students tended to describe themselves in their relationship to others: "I am a father of three boys" or "I have four living grandparents." "I am a member of a Presbyterian Church." Western students more often described themselves as individuals: "I am a soccer player." "I am a *Star Wars* fan." "I was born in Wisconsin." It was uncanny how cultural background influenced the way students described themselves as individuals or as members of a group.

I grew up in an individualistic culture where I was taught to debate ideas and think for myself. I remember how my dad grilled me one Sunday afternoon as I was preparing to leave home for college. I was driving our old red and white Chevrolet when my dad began to challenge me on my views of evolution. He asked me to make the case for evolution, and he would then counter with data that weakened my argument. After a while, he suggested that we switch sides. He would make the case for evolution and I was to challenge his ideas. In debate, I was taught to make a distinction between people and their ideas. I was taught to disagree with the person's ideas and still respect the individual. Dad wanted me to think for myself and not automatically accept the ideas of others. Challenging the ideas of others had become a game.

My dad was an individualist. He wore a bow tie even when they weren't in style. His clothes were often mismatched and rumpled, but he jokingly explained, "A handsome man looks good in anything." He didn't care what people thought about his clothes. His investment strategy was also contrarian. When everyone liked a company, he sold his stock. When everyone else thought the stock was bad, he would buy. His colleagues at the lab gave him a T-shirt emblazoned with the word *Iconoclast*. I wonder if my dad ever felt shamed because he wasn't paying attention to what others thought. I discovered later that my upbringing would have been unheard of in a collectivistic culture. No wonder I enjoy classes where students graciously disagree with me and the class discussion becomes intense.

In other cultures, children are raised to rely on the family and to be responsible for siblings. Extended families bind one another together through mutual obligation. Students help one another and expect to be helped by others in the class. This desire for harmony does not lend itself to debate in the classroom. Personal achievement is not for oneself but to bring honor to parents or to the reputation of the school.

The desire to avoid shaming family and friends is a powerful motivator in collectivistic cultures, and bringing honor to the group or the family is a high value. When students do well in school, their parents are honored. Behavior is guided by fear of shame rather than by personal guilt.[4]

Sometimes collectivism is found in individualistic cultures too. Collectivistic peer pressure is powerful among most American teens. There was a faction in my high school who thought it was uncool to study. A conscientious student might be greeted by jeers if seen carrying a textbook home. Such pressure can also lead to good outcomes, pushing students to success in athletics or the arts.

I personally needed to learn to be more flexible with cultural values. I grew up in a more individualistic culture. If I did poorly in school, I didn't worry about my parents being shamed in front of the neighbors. I may have felt personal guilt for being lax in my study habits, but I don't recall being ashamed. I chose my own university and informed my parents where I wanted to go. My wife and I met at college and I began dating her without consulting my parents or hers. I chose my academic major and my vocation without getting permission from my parents. I hope I made them proud, but doing so was more of an afterthought. I lived in a culture where my parents expected me to choose

---

[4]A helpful resource in further understanding honor and shame cultures is Jayson Georges and Mark D. Baker, *Ministering in Honor-Shame Cultures: Biblical Foundations and Practical Essentials* (Downers Grove, IL: InterVarsity Press, 2016).

a major, a wife, and a career without receiving permission from them. They intentionally taught me to be independent. Individualism has many strengths, but I'm afraid I missed out on the beauties of collectivism.

For most of my life I've been attempting to figure out when to shift gears so as to be more aware of the context, more respectful of power, more tolerant of ambiguity, and more appreciative of collectivistic values.

There are strengths and weaknesses in each of these cultural paradigms. Neither one is right or wrong, but the crosscultural teacher can gain intercultural competence by understanding differing cultural values. *Teaching across cultures requires the ability to shift styles and integrate educational paradigms.*

WHEN HUMILITY BACKFIRED

By Duane Elmer, professor emeritus of educational studies
at Trinity Evangelical Divinity School

In one of my overseas stints [in South Africa], I was the president of a Bible school. Working late on a Friday, I noticed the grass had not been cut. The church used our building on Sunday, and I was feeling a bit ashamed to have them come to a ragged-looking place. Everyone else had gone home, so I got out the lawn mower and cut the grass myself in my shirt and tie. The school was located on the border between a largely Indian community and another that was mostly mulatto or colored (mixed race). Being late in the afternoon, hundreds of people saw me laboring away. I must confess, I felt rather positive about the fact that I was modeling out humility before all these observing people. Surely my esteem would go up as the example of someone who did not consider himself above the menial.

The following Monday morning the students came to me confessing that they had forgotten their job and wondering how the grass got cut. I proudly announced that I did it, hoping that they too would see my humility. Noticing the glances of consternation they exchanged among themselves, I asked if anything was wrong. One of the senior students politely and gingerly announced that I had lost status before the entire community. "How can that be?" I fired back. "They saw you cutting the grass and believed that you had lost all authority in the school. You were not able to get any students to do it or any of your faculty or even your secretary." Furthermore, the school also lost credibility (remember collectivism?), because who can respect a place where everything is in chaos? After the shock wore off, I resolved to restore my status in the community and that of the school. For the next several months, I stood outside looking regal and authoritative while the students did their work.[5]

---

[5]Duane Elmer, *Crosscultural Connections: Stepping Out and Fitting In Around the World* (Downers Grove, IL: InterVarsity Press, 2002), 166-67.

7

TEACHING AIMS ACROSS CULTURES

Do not merely listen to the word, and so deceive yourselves.
Do what it says.

JAMES 1:22

You believe there is one God. Good!
Even the demons believe that—and shudder.

JAMES 2:19

THE ULTIMATE AIM of existence for every human being is to know and love God. The fundamental aim of education, then, in every culture is to foster the holistic development of persons into all God created them to become so they can know and love him. The astounding task of the teacher described in Ephesians is to equip people to become mature, "attaining to the whole measure of the fullness of Christ" (Eph 4:11-13).

Outward signs of maturity will look different in different cultures. Korean missionaries should not assume that mature believers in Bolivia will behave outwardly just like godly Koreans. For instance, the wonderful early morning prayer meetings with everyone simultaneously praying out loud that are integral to Korean churches may not be adopted by some cultures. Neither should New Zealanders assume that believers in India will adopt Western forms of worship. Yet Scripture does give us a general description of maturity.

The universal aim of teaching is to promote growth: "Then we will no longer be infants.... Instead, speaking the truth in love, we will grow to become in every respect the mature body of him who is the head, that is, Christ" (Eph 4:14-15).

Note the interdependent nature of individual and communal development. Individuals are to be built up into the body of Christ so that together they may attain to the fullness of Christ. Personal and communal development are like two sides of the same coin. If one aspect is missing, the coin is not genuine.

Complete maturity will not be achieved in this life. The apostle John reminds us, "Dear friends, now we are children of God, and what we will be has not yet been made known. But we know that when Christ appears, we shall be like him, for we shall see him as he is" (1 Jn 3:2). All of life is a journey toward becoming like Christ.

Though the aim of education is not fully accomplished in this life, our purpose as teachers is to promote maturity throughout the lifetime of the *pilgrim*. In contrast to the *gardener* model, we have an external purpose and direction outside of ourselves; and in contrast to the *production* model, there are unanticipated twists and turns in the journey. The pilgrim is on a lifetime journey with a visionary purpose, and the task of the teacher in any culture is to help guide that expedition.

As teachers, we work hard to promote small steps in the direction of maturity. While we may never see the final result, we can be encouraged when we see progress in the right direction. Development isn't automatic, and learning can't be forced any more than a forester can compel the growth of a sapling by pulling on it. Human development is from the inside out, not the top down. As teachers, we can nurture, encourage, and challenge growth, but we can't force it.

One of my small goals in teaching our church's junior boys Sunday school class was to help them see the Bible as exciting. One Sunday I had the boys do an inductive Bible study on the story of David and Goliath (1 Sam 17). Near the end, one boy leaned back in his chair, hit his hand on the side of his head, and enthusiastically exclaimed, "I never knew the Bible was so interesting!" I said to myself, *Yes*. This kid still had a long way to go in his appreciation of the Bible, but the Lord allowed me to see one small step in my desired direction. I never forgot this seemingly insignificant comment in our Sunday school class.

Even though it's not possible to see everything that is going on inside our students, most often we can detect indications of progress. *The teacher's aim is not a predetermined target but the nurturing of unpredictable progress in a desired general direction.*

HOLISTIC HUMAN DEVELOPMENT

I'm amazed that the King of the rulers of the earth and the Creator of millions of galaxies came into our world as a baby who needed to grow through the stages of development. He could have come as a full-grown man or as Superman or a Norse god of thunder!

Luke writes that "Jesus grew in wisdom and in stature and in favor with God and all the people" (Lk 2:52 NLT). There are multiple areas of growth, but surely these four are critical.

People grow as whole beings. Physical, mental, social, and spiritual development are intertwined. The four aspects of growth are in reality a single entity (see fig. 7.1). At the core of human development is spiritual growth in relationship with our Creator.

Schools often recognize the interdependence of the spiritual, physical, social, and intellectual. They seek to teach information while also fostering social and physical development, as students interact with teachers and with each other on the playground or lunch. In addition, Christian

Figure 7.1. Four aspects of human growth

schools seek to integrate the knowledge of God into all the curriculum.

Most of the time we grow gradually, almost imperceptibly. Our son probably doesn't recognize the gradual growth of our grandson, but when we grandparents see him after being apart for six months, we're surprised at how tall he's grown and how much he has changed. In the same way cognitive, spiritual, and social development may grow imperceptibly. But development also happens in growth spurts or stages. Let's look in more detail at these universal dimensions of development, concentrating on cognitive, spiritual, and social areas.

DIMENSIONS OF GROWTH

We are called to grow in favor with God: spiritual development is at the heart of all growth. We are called to "grow to become in every respect the mature body of him who is the head, that is, Christ" (Eph 4:15). One of the best descriptions of Christlikeness is a person who consistently displays the fruit of the Spirit: love, joy, peace, forbearance, kindness, goodness, faithfulness, gentleness, and self-control (Gal 5:22-23). While the outward expression of these qualities may look different in different cultures, the fruit of the Spirit embodies the core virtues that apply equally to any culture of the world. From a Christian perspective, they sum up what a life redeemed by God looks like.

The growth of our souls is the overarching theme of Scripture. The educational aims of the apostles Peter and Paul encompassed growth in faith, joy, grace, love, hope, and the knowledge of God. "We ought always to thank God for you, brothers and sisters, and rightly so, because your faith is growing more and more, and the love all of you have for one another is increasing" (2 Thess 1:3). Paul prayed for the fullness of joy for the church in Philippi (Phil 4:4), and Peter commanded his readers to *grow* in the grace of the Lord Jesus (2 Pet 3:18). Paul prayed for the Philippian Christians that their "love may abound more and more in knowledge and depth of insight" (Phil 1:9). He also prayed that his friends in Rome would "overflow with hope" (Rom 15:13). One of the best examples of the rail-fence model is seen in Paul's prayer for the Colossians that God would fill them "with the *knowledge of his will* through all the wisdom and understanding that the Spirit gives, so that you may *live a life worthy of the Lord* and please him in every way: bearing fruit in every good work, growing in the knowledge of God" (Col 1:9-10, italics added).

Spiritual development incorporates all of human development: growth in wisdom, stature, favor with God, and favor with others. God desires that we grow in *wisdom*, treating our *bodies* as his temple, growing in *love for God* and *love for one another*. The development of pilgrims as the aim of teaching demands that teachers focus on qualities rather than quantities, and that subject matter be a means, not an end.

We are called to grow in wisdom. The book of Proverbs often links wisdom with instruction and knowledge. "Fear of the LORD is the foundation of true knowledge" (Prov 1:7 NLT). Paul prays for believers to keep on growing in knowledge and understanding (Phil 1:9). Peter prays that believers will grow in grace and in the knowledge of our Lord and Savior Jesus Christ (2 Pet 3:18).

Knowledge is necessary for wisdom but insufficient on its own. Knowledgeable people can be quite unwise. True wisdom connects the knowledge of God with godly behavior. From the perspective of the rail-fence model, wisdom is exemplified by fence posts that connect the top rail of God's Word with the bottom rail of godly living.

We are called to grow in favor with people. Social development is included in the command to love our neighbor as ourselves (Mt 22:39). The church in Rome was encouraged to live in *peace* with everyone (Rom 12:18). The fruit of the Spirit leads to healthy interpersonal relationships with others through patience, kindness, goodness, faithfulness, and gentleness.

Teaching for holistic growth is a universal aim in education that is Christian.

THE AIM OF EDUCATION AND
THE ULTIMATE PURPOSE OF LIVING

While holistic development is the universal aim of education, it needs to move in a desired direction. Mere growth isn't the ultimate aim of human development. We must ask, "*Why* should people grow, and in what direction?" Educator John Dewey made the case that growth by itself is not an adequate aim for education.[1] He observed that students could develop into more effective burglars, gangsters, or corrupt politicians.[2] Individuals must have a purpose beyond themselves. Dewey ends his famous *Pedagogic Creed* with "I believe that in this way the teacher always is the prophet of the true God and the usherer in of the true kingdom of God."[3]

Growth for its own sake is insufficient and makes an idol out of the individual or society. From a biblical perspective we grow so we may know Christ and more fully bring glory to God. The apostle Paul expressed his ultimate aim in life: "I want to know Christ—yes, to know the power of his resurrection and participation in his sufferings, becoming like him in his death" (Phil 3:10).

Everything we teach should ultimately aim at helping the learner to increasingly love God and love others. The entire Bible is God's *special revelation*, offering grace and redemption for fallen humanity. Students can also grow in knowing God through the study of *general revelation* as understood through chemistry, astronomy, physics, literature, sociology, philosophy, anthropology, history, math, and education. The study of numbers, molecules, and galaxies can foster our love for the Creator, while an understanding of human relationships can help us love our neighbor as ourselves.

All this is in sharp contrast to the life goals of the average person. Our family sometimes played a board game called *Careers*. The object of the game was to fulfill one's goal in life—happiness, fame, or money. Players moved along the game board seeking occupations or experiences that would help to accomplish these goals. Later, a group of missionaries in Nigeria jokingly designed a similar game we called *Callings*. We could choose goals for collecting martyrdom points, ministry funds, image points, or status—all determined randomly by dice and a spinner. Both games show the shallowness of self-centered goals that don't focus

---

[1] John Dewey grew up in a Bible-believing home and spent much of his life teaching Sunday school. Later in life, his educational philosophy became naturalistic, but many of his principles still reflect his early upbringing.
[2] John Dewey, *Experience and Education* (New York: Collier Books, 1938), 36.
[3] John Dewey, "My Pedagogic Creed," *School Journal* 54 (January 1897): 80.

on a purpose and passion beyond ourselves. We are most fulfilled when our ultimate purpose in life will make a difference in eternity. It must be Godward, not inward.

New York Times columnist David Brooks writes that in order for people to deal with difficult times, they need a purpose for living. Without this purpose, they lack direction and live a fragile life. Brooks writes,

> If you really want people to be tough, *make them idealistic for some cause,* make them tender for some other person, make them committed to some worldview that puts today's temporary pain in the context of a larger hope. Emotional fragility seems like a psychological problem, but it has only a philosophical answer. People are really tough only after they have taken a leap of faith for some truth or mission or love.[4]

Jesus challenged his followers to "'Love the Lord your God with all your heart and with all your soul and with all your mind.' This is the first and greatest commandment. And the second is like it: 'Love your neighbor as yourself'" (Mt 22:37-39). Everything we teach—in every subject, to every student, and in every culture, should foster the development of persons into all God intended them to be so they will grow in their love for God and neighbor. Developmental teachers rejoice when they observe students making small steps on the path to maturity.

ONGOING LEARNING FOR TEACHING INTERCULTURALLY

By Grover Rebollo from Bolivia, working with Swiss camp personnel

Mirna came from Switzerland to Camp Kewina in Bolivia for six months to support specific camping programs. She wasn't experienced in camping but was studying international relations and language teaching in her country.

In the second month of her stay, we invited her to take the Christian Camping International course called "Building Relationships." Several of the concepts were difficult for her to assimilate, such as "Give love, affection, and empathy to the campers. Forge close relationships and talk intentionally with them." She questioned these directives, and this

---

[4]David Brooks, "Making Modern Toughness," *New York Times*, August 30, 2016, www.nytimes.com/2016/08/30/opinion/making-modern-toughness.html.

attitude made her feel isolated from the other counselors. She appreciated privacy for all, including the campers. For her, there was no justification for invading the rights and privacy of anyone, and these concepts in the course discouraged her.

How could we teach and demonstrate the richness of intentional camping relationships for her? We looked for ways to facilitate experiential moments in small groups, in the church, and in the camp so she could take part in all of this. After two months of observing, Mirna applied various guidelines from the course with the cabin leaders, but not with the campers. But she did come to have a sincere love for each person who came into her life, and she worked to create connections and networks to grow the team of Bolivian camp volunteers. When she returned to her country, she initiated a volunteer ministry to work with refugee families.

Sometimes, even unintentionally, we are teaching the values of our culture, beliefs, priorities, use of time, and how to cultivate relationships. This happens through formal and nonformal teaching, and all of this is part of the hidden curriculum that teaches far more than content.

The challenges and conflicts are also on our side as Bolivians. How do we learn, work and teach in an intercultural way? How can we come alongside one another and learn together? These are questions that have emerged and that continue to be addressed. In a crosscultural experience where you teach and then need to work with the students, there are many mistakes and successes on both sides. Learning has to be ongoing on the part of all.

CULTURAL INFLUENCES
ON TEACHING AIMS

If I could speak all the languages of earth and of angels,
but didn't love others, I would only be a noisy gong
or a clanging cymbal.

1 CORINTHIANS 13:1 NLT

THE BIBLE IS CLEAR that God's universal purpose for every person is to grow to love him with our whole being and to love our neighbor as ourselves. Yet this universal aim will take on distinct cultural flavors, and this is a good thing. While flexibility is important for those who teach people different from themselves, teachers must also commit to meeting common and eternal objectives. This dual commitment encourages teachers to adapt culturally without falling into cultural relativism. Not all cultural values promote the development of individuals in community. Radical individualism misses out on the benefits of the community and can lead to anarchy, while radical collectivism can dehumanize the individual (see table 8.1).

Table 8.1. Cultural values and educational aims

CULTURAL VALUE	EDUCATIONAL AIM
Collectivistic	Success for the sake of making family proud, avoiding shame, and bringing status and honor to the community.
Individualistic	Personal success in order to make money, make a name for oneself, and be happy.
High Tolerance for Ambiguity	Educational aims should be implicit and flow from the context.

Low Tolerance for Ambiguity	Educational aims must be precise, predictable, and quantifiable.
High Power Distance	Educational aims are whatever the teacher, school system, or community say they are.
Low Power Distance	Educational objectives must take into account the interests and desires of students.
High Context	Educational aims are flexible and relate to the changing needs of the everyday context.
Low Context	Educational aims are abstract and organized by academic disciplines, reflecting historic bodies of knowledge.

TYPES OF EDUCATIONAL AIMS

Elliott Eisner discusses three types of educational aims or aspirations: behavioral objectives, problem-solving objectives, and expressive outcomes.[1] While not discounting the occasional usefulness of behavioral objectives, Eisner pleads for a broader concept of teaching aspirations. He writes, "The dominant image of schooling in America has been the factory and the dominant image of teaching and learning the assembly line."[2]

Behavioral objectives. All around the world, examples of behavioral objectives are common in formal schooling. These aims must be formulated in advance with precision and stated in terms of observable performance for all students. Standardized testing is the main tool for evaluating whether the aims have been accomplished. Individual differences, needs, and interests of the learner are not taken into account in this type of aim.

When specific skills and competencies are necessary, behavioral objectives may be appropriate.[3] For example, I was once instructed by the elders of our church to make sure each boy in my Sunday school class could perfectly recite the Ten Commandments. The intended outcome was specific, predictable, observable, and related to the performance of the boys. I used a behavioral teaching method of positive reinforcement with candy bars to accomplish the task. Teaching a mechanic how to

---

[1]Elliot W. Eisner, *The Educational Imagination: On the Design and Evaluation of School Programs,* 3rd ed. (Columbus, OH: Merrill Prentice Hall, 2002), 108.
[2]Eisner, *Educational Imagination,* 361.
[3]Eisner, *Educational Imagination,* 113.

replace brakes on a car, a health care worker how to give an injection, or a soldier how to clean a rifle are examples of the usefulness of behavioral objectives.

Behavioral objectives are especially valued in low-context cultures with a low tolerance for ambiguity.

Problem-solving objectives. Problem-solving objectives are the second type of Eisner's outcomes. Teachers and students begin with a problem to be investigated with an unknown outcome. Since the solution is not known in advance, it can't be predictably quantified ahead of time.

Educational research is one example of a problem-solving activity. One begins with a practical problem, reviews the literature on the subject, and tests a hypothesis. The researcher does not know the outcome of the research at the beginning of the study.

The phenomenon of problem-based learning is becoming more common in educational circles. Cindy E. Hmelo-Silver describes the model in the *Educational Psychology Review*:

> Problem-based learning (PBL) is an instructional method in which students learn through facilitated problem solving. In PBL, student learning centers on a complex problem that does not have a single correct answer. Students work in collaborative groups to identify what they need to learn in order to solve a problem. . . . The teacher acts to facilitate the learning process rather than to provide knowledge.[4]

Theologizing is really a problem-solving activity. In the early church one practical problem concerned the nature of Christ. In Africa, one problem might center on the eternal state of ancestors or monogamous marriage. All of us come to theology with big questions and everyday concerns. We don't theologize with predetermined outcomes or prescribed educational activities.

Theological education by extension (TEE) was promoted by Ted Ward as a problem-solving activity. He intended the learning experience

---

[4]Cindy E. Hmelo-Silver, "Problem-Based Learning: What and How Do Students Learn?," *Educational Psychology Review* 16, no. 3 (September 2004): 235. For a helpful survey of problem-based learning, see Andrew Walker, Heather Leary, Cindy E. Hmelo-Silver, and Peggy A. Ertmer, eds., *Essential Readings in Problem-Based Learning* (West Lafayette, IN: Purdue University Press, 2015).

to connect the *field experience* of pastors with *cognitive input* from books or tape recordings. He pictured the teacher as the facilitator of an "integrative seminar" helping learners in community make connections between their felt need and the cognitive input. Ward eventually became disenchanted with TEE because of how it was misused as merely another technique for what he called "cognitive dumping."[5] Ward didn't intend TEE to be just an alternative teaching method but a paradigm shift in education. Too often missionaries adopted the method, but not the paradigm.

The rail-fence model builds on Eisner's problem-solving objectives. Problem solving begins in community with learners' bottom-rail questions. The teacher facilitates discovery of top-rail bodies of information that have the potential of solving the bottom-rail question. Since problem solving builds on the interests of the learner and moves to the learning of information, it has the potential of being acceptable in both high- and low-context cultures.

Expressive outcomes. Eisner's third type of educational aim is *expressive outcomes*. For example, a youth pastor might plan a winter trip for the youth group to the inner city in order to provide warm clothing to the homeless. The educational goal might be to provide an experience that helps high school students to better understand themselves, to gain empathy, and to affirm the dignity of the homeless. The intention of expressive outcomes is to provide rich experiences without a behavioral preplanned objective or the intention to solve a problem.

Art is a creative and expressive activity. Artists don't formulate precise objectives when they begin the creative work of forming a sculpture, composing a piece of music, or painting a watercolor. Worship is also an expressive outcome. Whether in private prayer or in communal praise music, the intended outcome is to express love for God.

Hall states, "Good art is always high-context, bad art, low-context."[6]

---

[5]Ted W. Ward, "Evaluating Metaphors of Education," in *With an Eye on the Future: Development and Mission in the 21st Century: Essays in Honor of Ted Ward*, ed. Duane Elmer and Lois McKinney (Monrovia, CA: MARC, 1996), 48.
[6]Edward T. Hall, *Beyond Culture* (Garden City, NY: Anchor Books, 1997), 92.

Cultural differences may predispose educational systems to prefer high- or low-context outcomes. High-context cultures with a high tolerance for ambiguity will likely prefer expressive or problem-solving outcomes, while low-context cultures with a low tolerance for ambiguity prefer behavioral objectives. Since the rail-fence model and the pilgrim metaphor include aspects of all three types of objectives, they are more likely to be appropriate to many cultures.

MEETING CULTURAL EXPECTATIONS

When I teach in another culture, it's important for me to understand the expectations of the students. I've experienced times when my desired teaching outcomes conflicted with the expectations of students, which is a situation that can lead to frustration and confusion for both teacher and students.

Here is one example. The Nigerian secondary school students looked bored as I explained a "most interesting" concept, so I was thrilled when a student in the back enthusiastically waved his hand. *Finally*, I thought, *I'm beginning to connect.* The student shattered my hopes by inquiring, "Will this be on the exam?" I then realized the disconnect between my educational aims for the class and those of the students. The goal of the students was to pass the government exam in order to gain a certificate and be accepted into the best university. I wanted to help students think for themselves and develop a curiosity for learning. The students were working within the educational system of the country and probably thought I was wasting their time and their chances for success in life. My initial instinct was to assume that the students were lazy and disrespectful, instead of realizing that my teaching was ineffective. I had not connected my objectives with those of the students. Later in the class I tried harder to demonstrate how my teaching aims could help them learn, and how these insights could improve their score on the exams. I'm not sure if they made the connection, but I realized that I needed to be more understanding and flexible. Unfortunately, this scenario plays out in both high- and low-context cultures as schools teach for the exam rather than teaching for life.

Another example might be a collectivistic village where the aim of education is to increase the status of the village. The village head values high power distance, decides to build a school, and requires all children to attend. Everything in the school should contribute to the status of the village—the qualifications of the teachers, the architecture of the school, and the curriculum. Graduates should be accepted into prestigious schools, resulting in high-paying jobs that will prepare them to come back and help the village.

A new teacher from another culture arrives with different cultural values. He aims to promote individual development by challenging students to think critically. The low power-distance teacher asks the students to call him by his first name. He encourages students to challenge him in class and jokes around with them after class. He even rides an undignified bicycle to class instead of arriving in a car.

Soon the students begin to use their critical reasoning to challenge the rules of the village leaders and stop showing respect for them. The unintentional mismatch of educational aims causes frustration and even anger for both the teacher and the village. Alarmed, the village runs the new teacher out.

HARMONIZING EXPECTATIONS

Harmonizing educational goals between teacher and students is critical for success in teaching. This is true in every setting, including the crosscultural challenge of intergenerational teaching.

Earlier I mentioned my class of eight-to-eleven-year-old boys in our Sunday school. My ultimate aim was to help the boys love God and neighbor, and to know and apply the Bible to their life needs. In contrast, the boys' expectation was to be cool, have fun, show off, and tune out of a boring lesson. The guys felt they were being forced to sit for an additional hour after already being quiet for an hour and a half in the worship service. When I walked in, two boys were wrestling on the floor and another was sitting with his head back, eyes closed, and snoring with a loud artificial snore. Two others were shooting spitballs at each other. What a mismatch! I didn't want to give up my intended outcomes, but God seemed to have programmed these guys with a desire to be cool and move around.

I tried to combine our aims, making the class as active as possible. We dramatized Bible stories and role-played the Bible teaching. I sheepishly admit that I bribed the boys by promising that if we finished the lesson early we would spend the last fifteen minutes playing soccer on the front lawn of the church. I'm sure mothers wondered how their boys got grass stains while studying the book of Mark, but the boys really did learn how to do inductive Bible studies and practiced application to their felt needs. They called themselves the FBI ("Faithful Bible Investigators"). We acted out the Bible story of Joshua fighting the Amalekites. (Unfortunately most of the boys wanted to be Joshua with the sword, and no one wanted to be Moses up on the hill praying.) I tried to help them to "be cool" in the eyes of their peers by affirming their thoughtful answers to challenging questions and by cheering them on in soccer. I'm not sure if we fully merged each other's aims, but we had fun and the guys learned to apply the Bible to their life challenges.

When I taught an evening course in adult education for a theological college in Ethiopia, I arrived early and chatted with students as they meandered in, asking them about their backgrounds and why they wanted to take this course. A couple students mentioned that this was the only course offered at this time and they needed to finish their MA quickly in order to get a raise in their job. My *intended outcome* was to facilitate a paradigm shift in an understanding of teaching and learning for adults. I hoped to help them see that the principles of adult nonformal education were more in line with traditional Ethiopian education than the schooling approach of memorizing facts for an exam. I spent most of the first class dialoguing with students about past meaningful and meaningless education in their lives and how their experiences fit the principles of adult learning. In that first class, I worked hard to facilitate a match between my intended outcomes and their intended outcomes for the class. But I also wanted to enlarge their vision to sense the life-changing possibilities of a different educational paradigm.

CONFLICT OF OBJECTIVES

The conflict of educational objectives is one of the causes for the radical Islamic Boko Haram movement in northeastern Nigeria. The word *boko* usually means "Western education," but it can also mean "fraud" or "trick," and *haram* can mean "unlawful" or "forbidden" by Islamic law. The dominant group in the far northeast of Nigeria are the Kanuri people. Alan Peshkin wrote a classic educational monograph titled *Kanuri School Children: Education and Social Mobilization in Nigeria.*[7] His study may shed light on the tensions today.

Peshkin and his Nigerian students followed four Kanuri school children and their families for a month, recording connections between the school, the community, and the home. The most common motivation for parents sending their children to a Western school was so they could earn more money and support their parents in old age. He observes, "Daily classroom experiences were not calculated to have much immediate impact on a child's life either in his public or private roles. That is, he was not intentionally instructed to consider either new goals or new ways of thinking, improving his society or ordering his life."[8] Peshkin observed that the hidden curriculum of Western schooling was to allow children to reject their father's occupation and promote independence that weakened kinship ties.[9] Western education subtly undercut traditional values and was also disconnected from the realities of the community and the home. He writes,

> Students receive "scientific" explanations for the body's organs and in-structions for purifying water and eliminating malaria-bearing mosquitoes. Such explanations are applicable for school examination purposes, but they are difficult to internalize. Indeed, interviews with more recent graduates from Maiduguri's secondary school suggests that they reject classroom knowledge that conflicts with traditional knowledge. When asked about their five years of science instruction, the graduates claimed

---

[7]Alan Peshkin, *Kanuri Schoolchildren: Education and Social Mobilization in Nigeria* (Chicago: Holt, Rinehart & Winston, 1972).
[8]Peshkin, *Kanuri Schoolchildren*, 18.
[9]Peshkin, *Kanuri Schoolchildren*, 133.

they know the "correct" answers for examination purposes but could not accept them as fact.[10]

One wonders if the Nigerian Boko Haram conflict today might have been avoided if the objectives of Western education made a greater attempt to meld with the needs of traditional Kanuri society.

While serving in Nigeria, I traveled with Nigerian church leaders to conduct seminars on the educational role of the local church. We visited about twenty district church councils. Pastor Philip Gambo, Rev. David Buremoh, Rev. Samuila Kure, and I gave passionate lectures with solid exposition from Scripture on the responsibility of the local church not just to preach but to teach every age level. Along with teaching important concepts, we sang animated Hausa choruses about the importance of being on time for Sunday school. One chorus was about a turtle who was always late for Sunday school and how it should instead be like rabbits who arrived on time. At the end of the seminar local pastors and district church leaders were enthusiastic about our time together. But the chorus made little difference on punctuality.

The next year we continued seminars in each of the church districts. We found that most pastors didn't do any of the assignments we had asked them to do the year before. If we were such good teachers, why were our seminars such a disappointment? My guess is that there was a mismatch in cultural values between our intended outcomes and the reason the pastors attended our seminar.

If we are to become more effective crosscultural teachers, we must be aware of our own implicit and explicit educational values *as well as* those of the learners.

CREDENTIALS: THE EXPECTED AIM OF EDUCATION

Another incongruity between the aims of teachers and students is what we may consider real learning versus merely teaching for educational credentials.

---

[10]Peshkin, *Kanuri Schoolchildren*, 136.

The following story is common in much of the world. A young boy does well in the village primary school and passes the entrance exam for the regional secondary school There he excels and does well in the entrance exam for university. As he graduates from university he is given a well-paying job and soon returns to his village driving a big black Mercedes Benz automobile. Suddenly, all the parents in the village want their children to go to school. Passing tests becomes the formula for gaining wealth in order to support parents. Schooling is no longer about learning skills that are useful for farming, hunting, cooking, village politics, or family heritage. The *diploma disease* takes over when education for credentials replaces education for life.[11]

This pressure to pass exams has permeated the globalized village. Many Korean students get up early to study, spend all day in school, and then go to cram schools or *hagwons* after school until 10 p.m. or even later. Se-Woong Koo writes that South Korea's educational system hurts students.

> The world may look to South Korea as a model for education—its students rank among the best on international education tests—but the system's dark side casts a long shadow. Dominated by Tiger Moms, cram schools and highly authoritarian teachers, South Korean education produces a rank of overachieving students who pay a stiff price in health and happiness. The entire program amounts to child abuse.[12]

Koo points out that the modern exam system in Korea is not simply a product of Western education but is based on an ancient system for preparing for civil service exams. These were administered by the royal court as far back as 1392. Passing the exams would assure families of financial success and social status. Parents decided the educational aspirations of their children. "To be a South Korean child ultimately is not about freedom, personal choice or happiness; it is about production, performance and obedience."[13]

---

[11]Ronald Dore, *The Diploma Disease: Education, Qualification and Development* (London: Institute of Education of London, 1997).
[12]Se-Woong Koo, "An Assault upon Our Children: South Korea's Educational System Hurts Students," *New York Times*, August 1, 2014, www.nytimes.com/2014/08/02/opinion/sunday/south-koreas-education-system-hurts-students.html.
[13]Koo, "Assault upon Our Children."

For much of the world, including the United States, the most common aim of education is to pass a decontextualized standardized test. The challenge of the crosscultural teacher is to help students pass exams while also relating the content of the exam to the practical questions faced by students. We can aid students in passing exams while also helping them realize the useful nature of the material they are learning.

Cultural values powerfully influence expected educational objectives. Effective crosscultural teachers are aware of different expectations even as they attempt to broaden them.

LEARNING FROM AN AWKWARD INTERRUPTION

By Lisa Anderson Umaña from the United States, teaching in Latin America

I stood at the whiteboard, marker in hand, writing out the agenda of the day's training. All were seated, watching attentively, when suddenly the door opened wide and in walked a latecomer. All eyes turned to him as he began to make his way around the room, greeting each person in turn, a handshake for the men and a kiss on the cheek for the women.

I couldn't help but feel my jaw drop as I stood in stunned silence, unable to say a word. My mind struggled to comprehend what was happening. As he neared the end of the row of fellow students, he turned to me with a smile and a nod, and sat in the chair provided for him by his classmates.

All eyes returned to me as I searched for words to continue. I mumbled something about the importance of punctuality and continued writing on the board to distract myself from my rising sense of irritation.

After class, I pondered what happened: He was thirty minutes late but felt no apparent shame in being tardy. He did not slink in but rather boldly interrupted my class as he greeted everyone. No one chided him for his tardiness but rather responded joyfully to his greeting of each individual. They even offered him a seat in the front.

Later, I discovered he was a pastor, a person of high status in Mexico. At that point in my missionary career, I had no idea of the cultural dimension of high power distance and its implications. I was upset that he was unapologetically late, had shamelessly interrupted my class, and usurped the attention of the students with his greetings. I had no idea of the cultural value in Latin America of showing respect for the dignity of each person.

I read the situation exclusively through the eyes of my North American cultural grid that places a high value on punctuality—so much so that an apology is expected for lateness, accompanied by some sign of remorse and causing as little interruption as possible to others around you.

Years went by before I studied Geert Hofstede's cultural dimensions and made sense of numerous awkward moments as I finally attributed them properly to differences in cultural values. I only wish I had studied culture sooner, at the beginning of my missionary career.

9

TEACHING THROUGH STRUGGLE

*Consider it pure joy, my brothers and sisters, whenever you face trials
of many kinds, because you know that the testing of your faith produces
perseverance. Let perseverance finish its work
so that you may be mature and complete,
not lacking anything.*

JAMES 1:2-4

To get lost is to learn the way.

SWAHILI PROVERB

Give advice. If people don't listen, let adversity teach them.

ETHIOPIAN PROVERB

THE FRUSTRATIONS OF LIFE are the driving force behind human
development. The struggle may be physical, intellectual, spiritual, or
interpersonal. It's true that we learn some things that don't come through
struggle, but seldom do these things stimulate development. A person
becomes better at chess or tennis only when they play people better
than themselves. Only through struggle does one improve.

The struggle may be a perplexing situation, a problem, a frustration, or
merely a life situation that doesn't make sense. In this world, we live with
inherent tension, tension between the way things are and the way they
should be, between what God wants us to do and what we want to do,
between the top rail of God's truth and the bottom rail of our lives. When

we live in harmony with the will of God, we are in a state of equilibrium. When we ignore the clear teaching of Scripture, we live in a state of painful disequilibrium. At times, through no personal fault of our own, God allows painful experiences to enter our lives—the death of a loved one, the slow agony of cancer, or the loss of property through hurricanes, floods, or fire.

BIBLICAL EXAMPLES

From a biblical and developmental perspective, struggle is the stimulus for growth. God promises to not tempt us beyond what we are able to bear, but will make a way of escape that we may be able to endure the trial (1 Cor 10:13). The reasons for suffering are usually a mystery we will never understand in this world, but at least one purpose of testing is to develop us into God's purposes for us.

The faith of Abraham was sorely tested when God commanded him to sacrifice his son Isaac (Gen 22:2). Abraham trusted the promises of God to such an extent that he knew God could raise Isaac from the dead (Heb 11:19). Through the struggle of deciding to trust God or give up his most valuable possession, Abraham chose to trust. God spared Isaac, and Abraham grew in his faith. God tested Job with the loss of everything he held dear: his children, his wealth, and his health, yet Job declared, "He knows the way that I take; / when he has tested me, I will come forth as gold" (Job 23:10). The psalmist understood the purpose of testing. "For you, God, tested us; / you refined us like silver" (Ps 66:10).

The turning point in Jacob's life was the night he wrestled with God. Jacob was facing the possibility that his brother, Esau, might massacre him and his family. He divided his family on two sides of a stream and spent the night alone. During the night, "a man wrestled with him till daybreak" (Gen 32:24). At daybreak, neither could overcome the other, and Jacob agreed to let the man go if he would bless him. The man changed Jacob's name from *cheater* to Israel, meaning *he struggles with God* (Gen 32:28). Struggle was the stimulus for Jacob's development.

The apostle Paul encouraged the Christians in Rome to join him in his struggle through prayer (Rom 15:30). He reminded the Ephesian church that "our struggle is not against flesh and blood, but against the rulers, against the authorities, against the powers of this dark world and against the spiritual forces of evil in the heavenly realms" (Eph 6:12). James reminds us that "the testing of your faith produces perseverance. Let perseverance finish its work so that you may be mature and complete (Jas 1:2-4).

Jesus consistently caused disequilibration in his hearers with sayings and parables they didn't understand. "It is easier for a camel to go through the eye of a needle than for someone who is rich to enter the kingdom of God" (Mk 10:25). He said, love your enemy, turn the other cheek, blessed are the poor in spirit, you must be born again. The disciples wondered, *Are we really supposed to love our enemies? Why does Jesus offend the religious leaders by healing on the Sabbath? What does he mean by the yeast of the Pharisees?* Most of Jesus' teaching was unexpected and often confusing. Jesus' teaching compelled struggle that deepened faith.

Personal Examples

I suspect that the majority of the things I've learned over the years have been forgotten. The ones that stuck grew out of the struggle to solve a difficulty or dilemma. In my youth I struggled with the conundrum of predestination and free will. These two seemed impossible to reconcile, and both were found in the Bible. Was the Bible mistaken? Could I lose my salvation? Could I sin all I wanted and still be saved? As a child, our family attended a Presbyterian church. I took notes during the sermons and was often comforted by remembering that God is sovereignly in control of the universe. In my teen years, we moved and began attending an old-time Methodist church. The preaching was demonstrative and came with frequent invitations to kneel and pray at the railing by the pulpit. I enjoyed both churches, but the difference in their theology confused me. I remember staying up late at night arguing with my friends on the questions of predestination. I think I switched positions every year or two, and was genuinely puzzled about this theological dilemma. How could both be true, and what should I believe? I could argue with Bible verses for either side.

Later, in graduate school, I took a course on historical theology, exploring theological debates that had taken place over the centuries. I had writer's cramp after each class from attempting to write down everything the professor said. Today I can't remember much of what he taught except for one story that shed light on my teenage dilemma. The professor described the unusual relationship between John Wesley, a strong believer in free will, and George Whitefield, an ardent Calvinist. Even though the two had heated disagreements, they worked together in evangelism. It struck me that if two great minds in theology couldn't agree on how to solve my question, who was I to discover a simple solution. I was sobered to realize that there are some things that will remain a mystery until we get to heaven. Fifty years later I remember this lecture because it helped me resolve a long, personal struggle and influenced me in broader areas of theology that are puzzling to our finite minds.

When I teach a course on crosscultural communication, I often begin by asking students, "What is the most important thing you've learned in life?" After hearing their responses, I ask, "How did you learn this?" By far the most common responses reflect struggle. "We didn't have enough money." "My best friend died in a car crash." "I didn't get the job I really wanted." "My dreams were shattered." In story after story, my students illustrate the point that the most powerful learning comes through difficulty. We learn most profoundly when life's struggles drive us to seek answers. This is the kind of learning that promotes the development of pilgrims.

I have often assigned readings I disagree with, such as the behaviorist book *Beyond Freedom and Dignity* by B. F. Skinner. Most of the students strongly disagreed with the book, but when I inquired about how they ran an evening children's program in their church, they realized that they were using Skinnerian principles to motivate good behavior, attendance, and Bible memory. Reflection on the connection between the book and the children's program resulted in a disequilibrating intellectual struggle.

EDUCATIONAL EXAMPLES

The role of struggle in education for promoting the growth of the learner is a common theme among significant educators. We'll look briefly at Jean Piaget, C. S. Lewis, John Dewey, George MacDonald, and Paulo Freire.

Jean Piaget. One of the most influential developmental psychologists of the last century was Jean Piaget, who generated important studies on the factors that promote development.[1] Two important factors are *social interaction* and the process of *exploring tensions* or disequilibration. People tend to grow and develop as they struggle with problems in groups.[2] His theories have been supported and refined by hundreds of crosscultural studies.

According to Piaget, people make the most cognitive progress in their thinking when things don't make sense. For example, little Billy, a small child, may have a single mental category for animals—his family dog. Everything with four legs, a tail, and a wet nose is a dog. When Billy sees his neighbor's cat with four legs, a kind of tail, and a sort of wet nose, Billy identifies the cat as a dog. This continues until Billy sees a cow. The cow has the characteristics of a dog, yet is very different. The cow doesn't quite fit the mental category of a dog, and this causes disequilibration. The puzzling situation prompts Billy to construct a broader mental category of animals, and leads to what Piaget identifies as cognitive development.[3] Piaget's theory of disequilibration and social interaction supports the journey metaphor of pilgrims facing difficulties as they travel together.

Piaget's theory applies to adults as well. Adults also grow as they explore tensions that create new categories, and this process is enhanced though interaction with others. This means that small groups can provide an ideal setting for healthy growth. For example, when a Presbyterian and a Pentecostal struggle together over the Pentecost passage in Acts 2, it's possible that healthy disequilibration will take place. As they explore the tensions of their differences in interpretation, both will see things they never saw before in that passage. Interaction with people who have different perspectives can be a powerful stimulus to grow.

---

[1]This section is modified from Jim and Carol Plueddemann, *Pilgrims in Progress: Growing Through Groups* (Wheaton, IL: Harold Shaw, 1990), 33-34.

[2]Jean Piaget and Bärbel Inhelder, *The Psychology of the Child* (New York: Basic Books, 1969).

[3]The example is adapted from James E. Plueddemann, "The Power of Piaget," in *Nurture That Is Christian: Developmental Perspectives on Christian Education*, ed. James C. Wilhoit and John M. Dettoni (Wheaton, IL: Victor Books, 1995), 51.

C. S. Lewis. C. S. Lewis struggled with the problem of pain. He wrote, "If God were good, He would wish to make His creatures perfectly happy, and if God were almighty He would be able to do what He wished. But the creatures are not happy. Therefore God lacks either goodness, or power, or both."[4] Lewis concluded that one of the reasons for pain is to help us hear God. "God whispers to us in our pleasures, speaks in our conscience, but shouts in our pains: it is His megaphone to rouse a deaf world."[5]

John Dewey. During his lifetime John Dewey significantly influenced education in America and was invited to give lectures in the Soviet Union and China. John Dewey grew up in a Christian home. When he was a child, his mother helped him memorize Bible verses, and for many years as a professor he also taught Sunday school. Though he distanced himself from his earlier beliefs later in life, his educational theories have been helpful to many Christian educators. His book *Experience and Education*, written near the end of his career, summarized his passion for integrating the experiences of the child with what he called "the funded capital of civilization."[6] Dewey insisted that *problems* growing out of the present experiences of the learner were incentives for learning.

> Problems are the stimulus to thinking. . . . Growth depends on the presence of difficulty to be overcome by the exercise of intelligence. Once more, it is part of the educator's responsibility to see equally two things: First, that the problem grows out of the conditions of the experiences being had in the present, and that it is within the range of the capacity of students; and secondly, that it is such that it arouses in the learner an active quest of information and for production of new ideas.[7]

For Dewey the problems of life were the stimulus for development as students connected the top-rail subject matter with their bottom-rail experiences.

George MacDonald. George MacDonald is best known for his fantasy writing, which influenced the thinking of C. S. Lewis, J. R. R. Tolkien,

---

[4]C. S. Lewis, *The Problem of Pain* (London: Fontana Books, 1959), 14.
[5]Lewis, *Problem of Pain*, 81.
[6]John Dewey, "My Pedagogic Creed," *School Journal* 54 (January 1897): 77.
[7]John Dewey, *Experience and Education* (New York: Collier, 1938), 79.

Lewis Carroll, W. H. Auden, Madeleine L'Engle, and many other writers. Much of his writing incorporates an educational theme, including the story of *The Wise Woman*. The story is about two spoiled, selfish girls— Rosemond, a princess, and Agnes, the daughter of a poor shepherd. Through a long and frustrating process of teaching and tasks, both girls were eventually taught to be kind and unselfish. The wise woman's educational approach was to give the girls a simple assignment, such as cleaning the cottage, and then leaving them alone to carry out the assignment. At first the girls failed the task, so the wise woman allowed them to face the consequences of their failure and kindly instructed them on how to improve the next time. Throughout this process the wise woman showed firm and loving patience. Each step of the developmental process involved a struggle to do the right thing when the natural inclination was to do the wrong thing. When princess Rosemond began to grow into a lovely person, the wise woman challenged her with the test of a "mood chamber." The wise woman said,

> "Rosemond, if you would be a blessed creature instead of a mere wretch, you must submit to be tried."
>
> "Is that something terrible?" asked the princess, turning white.
>
> "No, my child; but it is something very difficult to come well out of. Nobody who has not been tried knows how difficult it is, but whoever has come well out of it . . . always looks back with horror, not on what she has come through, but on the very idea of the possibility of having failed, and being still the same miserable creature as before."[8]

The wise woman began teaching with the bottom-rail needs of Rosemond and Agnes, and gave them top-rail instruction on how to complete the assigned task. She then worked with them as they struggled to discover fence-post connections between the teaching and their obedience. This teaching approach eventually fostered the developmental process of helping Rosemond and Agnes to becoming beautiful, unselfish human beings.

---

[8]George MacDonald, *The Wise Woman and Other Stories* (1875; repr., Grand Rapids: Eerdmans, 1980), 81-82.

Paulo Freire. While Paulo Freire is a controversial figure because of his influence on Latin American liberation theology, I find many aspects of his teaching to be in line with biblical principles.[9] Freire had deep compassion for the poor and oppressed in Brazil. As an educator, he discovered that the felt need of the oppressed was to learn to read, but the deeper need for them was to become self-confident human beings with an awakened consciousness so as to influence society. Freire was opposed to what he called the banking theory of education, where teachers deposit bodies of information into passive heads. In contrast he promoted the idea of "culture-circles."

> Through this project, we launched a new institution of popular culture, a "culture-circle," since among us a school was a traditionally passive concept. Instead of a teacher, we had a coordinator; instead of lectures, dialogue; instead of pupils, group participants; instead of alienating syllabi, compact programs that were "broken down" and "codified into learning units."[10]

Freire began with the bottom-rail need of learning how to read. Then in dialogue with the learners he generated top-rail pictures, words, and syllables that represented problem-posing situations for the oppressed. Through dialogue in culture circles, they learned how to read in record time and also began to take pride in themselves, their work, and their ability to influence society.

Struggle is a universal incentive for learning and a stimulus for human development. A challenging situation is the starting point that can lead to a desire for information. This in turn leads to a solution that meets a growth-producing deeper need, not merely the original felt need.

The primary function of the teacher then, in any culture, is to help students identify personal disequilibrating experiences and relate these to helpful information. This educational process has the potential of promoting human development.

Growing into Christlikeness is not accomplished through an educational technique alone but through a supernatural developmental process.

---

[9]Paulo Freire's most well-known book is *Pedagogy of the Oppressed* (New York: Seabury Press, 1968).

[10]Paulo Freire, *Education for Critical Consciousness* (New York: Continuum, 1982), 42.

As Judith and Sherwood Lingenfelter remind us, "Biblical transformation involves suffering, repentance, commitment, and practice doing what Jesus has commanded. The classroom is the least effective place for this to occur."[11] The teacher can do everything right and still not produce spiritual development. The Holy Spirit is the ultimate teacher working through spiritually gifted teachers who connect the Word of God with human needs in such a way that leads to growth.

GRACIOUS DISEQUILIBRATING DIALOGUE

By Jack Robinson, professor at Bangui Evangelical
School of Theology, Central African Republic, retired

I decided recently to leave a small group that I had been a part of for over a decade. The people are good friends, but our studies together weren't connecting with where we were living. We avoided talking about controversial or sensitive issues because we didn't want to create divisions. So, our thoughts and feelings about important subjects remained hidden. I didn't want to spend more time on this very familiar ground any longer, but decided to give it one more try.

When we reassembled, I made a radical proposal. "We've just finished two years reading through Luke's Gospel, and we've also discussed good books. What would you think if this year we make up our own agenda as we go along? We could discuss a different topic each week based on a subject somebody really wants to talk about. We could discuss controversial

issues, delicate issues, and subjects that we know we don't agree on. Why don't we go at the toughest issues we can think of, the ones we can get excited or angry about because they are really important to us?"

That's when people's eyes started getting big. I just kept talking. "How about discussing homosexuality? Or political polarization? What do you fear the most that you are willing to talk about? What are your greatest hopes for the future? And how does your Christian faith influence your thinking and behavior on all of these questions?"

I could feel both interest and skepticism in the room. Would changing the character of our discussions so radically actually work? Some sort of ground rules would surely be necessary. After talking it over we ended up with three guidelines.

---

[11]Judith E. Lingenfelter and Sherwood G. Lingenfelter, *Teaching Cross-Culturally: An Incarnational Model for Learning and Teaching* (Grand Rapids: Baker Academic, 2003), 98.

First, arguing the superiority of one point of view over against another would be off-limits. Arguing was out. Second, our positive goal would be to listen to one another and try to learn from one another, not to debate. Third, when a person wanted to describe their position on an issue, they needed to tell a story. The story would be about the experiences that led them to the position they were describing. Our goal would be to listen, to learn, to have our thinking stretched, and to grow as a result.

In the end, we decided to give it a try. As we shared our personal feelings and beliefs with one another, a sense of deeper connection began to develop. We found it safe to disclose our thoughts, even on sensitive issues, and felt a new appreciation and respect developing.

Many services and classes in the church are built around one-way communications. But people want to talk about how their faith and the realities of life come together or how they conflict. We need a chance to express what is going on in our minds and hearts as we wrestle with tough issues. As we listen to one another, we try to figure out how we as individuals want to live and grow as followers of Jesus. It is proving to be a refreshing and transformative experience for us all.

10

HARMONY THROUGH
THE RAIL-FENCE MODEL

One mark of a great educator is the ability to lead students out
to new places where even the educator has never been.

THOMAS GROOME

THE RAIL-FENCE MODEL harmonizes two competing educational
ideologies: should we teach the subject matter, or should we
teach students?[1]

A popular top-rail view of education championed by E. D. Hirsch Jr.
emphasizes mastering subject matter. He argues that the problem with
today's schools is that they are too *student centered*, stressing life relevance
over mastering bodies of knowledge. He writes in *The Schools We Need
and Why We Don't Have Them* that the reason American schools fail
so miserably in international comparisons is because of progressive
education with "anti-subject matter theories" of teaching.[2] What schools
need, he says, is the teaching of core knowledge through memory and
repetition. His ideas are an example of the *production* metaphor of education. We've seen that the teaching of core knowledge is necessary but
not sufficient for promoting human development.

At the other end of the spectrum is the bottom-rail *romantic* ideology
of child-centered education. Radical advocates of this approach are
opposed to social control and desire individual freedom for the child.
In his famous description of the Summerhill School, A. S. Neill writes,

---

[1]James E. Plueddemann, "Do We Teach the Bible or Do We Teach Students?," *Christian Education Journal* 10, no. 1 (Autumn 1986): 73-81.
[2]E. D. Hirsch Jr., *The Schools We Need and Why We Don't Have Them* (New York: Anchor Books, 1996).

"How can happiness be bestowed? My own answer is: Abolish authority. Let the child be himself. Don't push him around. Don't teach him. Don't lecture him. Don't elevate him. Don't force him to do anything."[3]

While the Summerhill example may be extreme, the fundamental principle is the same as Rousseau's, who argued that human development comes from the inside. He writes in *Emile*, "God makes all things good; man meddles with them and they become evil."[4] Rousseau desired to isolate the child Emile from the world, providing a tutor who would allow the child to grow according to his nature. Neill and Rousseau are classic examples of the *gardener* metaphor taken to its extreme.

While it's vital to take into account the needs and interests of the student, the exclusive student-centered emphasis that ignores the top rail of important bodies of knowledge is hazardous. The rail-fence model harmonizes content-centered education with student-centered education and overcomes the inadequacy of one without the other.

John Dewey summarized the dilemma by bringing together the curriculum and the student: "The history of educational theory is marked by opposition between the idea that education is development from within and that it is formation from without."[5] He argued for *interaction* between the subject matter, identified as the "funded experience of the past," and the experience of the child.[6] His educational theory was neither subject-matter-centered nor child-centered, but focused on integration between the two. Dewey often used the metaphor of journey and the importance of maps to guide experience.[7] The subject matter of the map provided guidance for the development of the learner.

Through careful observation, Jean Piaget found that children truly learn when they are actively involved in inventing meaning. In his book *To Understand Is to Invent*, he writes, "The goal of intellectual education is not to know how to repeat or retain ready-made truths (a truth that

---

[3]A. S. Neill, *Summerhill* (New York: Hart, 1960), 297.
[4]Jean-Jacques Rousseau, *Emile*, trans. Barbara Foxley (1778; repr., London: J. M. Dent, 1778), 1.
[5]John Dewey, *Experience and Education* (New York: Collier, 1938), 17.
[6]Dewey, *Experience and Education*, 42-43.
[7]John Dewey, *The Child and the Curriculum* (Chicago: University of Chicago Press, 1902), 19-20.

is parroted is only a half-truth). It is in learning to master the truth by oneself at the risk of losing a lot of time and of going through all the roundabout ways that are inherent in real activity."[8]

As children incorporate concepts into their way of thinking, they "invent" understanding. Any other kind of learning is short-lived. Piaget writes that most people forget the things they've learned in school if they only memorize the concept without understanding it. He critiques traditional schools that teach "intellectual gymnastics" with soon forgotten memorized facts such as the definition of a cosine, rules for the fourth Latin conjugation, or dates of military history.[9] Children invent unforgettable meaning when they make connections between their experience and the subject matter.

The rail-fence model brings together student-centered and content-centered ideologies of education. Mastering bodies of knowledge is absolutely necessary in the model, but not in isolation from the experience of the learner. Rigorous academic study is an integral aspect of the rail-fence model and may at times call for meaningful memorization.

EXAMPLES FROM CHRISTIAN EDUCATORS

Christian educators struggle with the same dilemma: Do we teach the Bible or do we teach students?[10]

Lois LeBar, one of my professors, taught the "boy-book-boy" model.[11] Teachers should begin with the felt needs of the "boy," link these felt needs to the book, God's Word, and then help the boy make a connection between the book and his real needs. She showed how Jesus began with the felt needs of his learners and then took them to the truth of the living Word, challenging them to make the connection between truth and life. She often quoted John 14:6: "Jesus answered, 'I am the way [bottom rail] and the truth [top rail] and the life [bottom

---

[8]Jean Piaget, *To Understand Is to Invent: The Future of Education* (New York: Grossman, 1973), 106.

[9]Piaget, *To Understand Is to Invent*, 93.

[10]Plueddemann, "Do We Teach the Bible?," 73.

[11]Lois E. LeBar and James E. Plueddemann, *Education That Is Christian* (Colorado Springs, CO: David C. Cook, 1995), 100.

rail]." Jesus knew that the surface felt needs of learners were seldom their real or deeper needs, and that he, the living Word, resolved the deepest needs.

LeBar cited John Amos Comenius as an example of an educator with a theory of education that harmonized the needs of the child with the information to be taught. Comenius integrated insights from "God's written revelation and from his second book of nature."[12] His major work was titled *The Great Didactic: Setting Forth the Whole Art of Teaching All Things to All Men*.[13] He emphasized the importance of promoting the development of the child from within. The incentive for learning, he said, should be the intrinsic interest of the child. The foundation of knowledge was the firsthand experience of the child. Teaching should guide the child rather than push them to what he called, "storing the memory."[14]

Another of my professors was Larry Richards, who modified the LeBar model to "hook, book, look, took."[15] The teacher begins with a felt need to *hook* the interest of the students, which leads to the study of the *book*, the Bible. The students then *look* at how truth is related to life, leading to the *took* part of the lesson where the students contemplate action. Note again the fence-post connection between the interests and needs of the learner that lead to a study of the subject matter and result in developed experiences.

My wife and I were delighted when Professor Thomas Groome stayed at our home while he gave lectures at Wheaton College. His book *Christian Religious Education* shed a fresh light from a Catholic perspective on the integration of truth and life. He wrote of five movements for shared practice: (1) name present action, (2) share participants' stories and visions, (3) share the story and vision of the Christian community, (4) explore the dialectic between the story of the community and the participants' stories, and (5) explore the dialectic between

---

[12]LeBar and Plueddemann, *Education That Is Christian*, 48.
[13]See LeBar and Plueddemann, *Education That Is Christian*, 50.
[14]John Amos Comenius, quoted in LeBar and Plueddemann, *Education That Is Christian*, 52.
[15]Lawrence O. Richards and Gary J. Bredfeldt, *Creative Bible Teaching* (Chicago: Moody Press, 1970), 160.

the vision of the community and the vision of the participants.[16] His model pointed out the fence post of dialectical tension or praxis between the bottom-rail stories of the learner and the top-rail story of the community.

All three of these Christian educators reflect the rail-fence model introduced by my doctoral mentor Ted Ward. They begin with the experiences and felt needs of the learners, take the learners to the subject matter of the Bible and the church, and then challenge the learners to make the connection between truth and life. Learning that promotes human development is enhanced by reflection and action on truth and experience.

Examples from the Bible

The Bible is filled with examples of how God uses puzzling life-related situations to foster our development. Here are five.

Nicodemus. Jesus flummoxed Nicodemus by teaching that no one could see the kingdom of God unless they were born again. Confused, Nicodemus exclaimed, "Surely they cannot enter a second time into their mother's womb to be born!" (Jn 3:3). Jesus began with questions and then moved to answers. He didn't immediately tell Nicodemus how to be born again but aroused his curiosity and stimulated him to ask leading questions. Jesus began with Nicodemus's question and helped him to relate new information to his original inquiry.[17]

Samaritan woman. Jesus caused disequilibrium in the Samaritan woman at the well by offering her living water so she would thirst no more. She took him literally and said, "Sir, give me this water so that I won't get thirsty and have to keep coming here to draw water" (Jn 4:15). He used her initial disequilibrium to compel deeper reflection and understanding about himself. This led her to believe in Jesus as the Messiah and then to bring her whole village to hear him.

---

[16]Thomas H. Groome, *Christian Religious Education: Sharing Our Story and Vision* (San Francisco: Harper, 1980), 207-22.

[17]The ideas in this paragraph are taken from Jim Plueddemann and Carol Plueddemann, *Pilgrims in Progress: Growing Through Groups* (Wheaton, IL: Harold Shaw, 1990), 57.

Jesus never taught by rote memory and seldom gave tidy explanations for what he taught. He challenged his hearers to struggle with his teachings so the truth would sink in and change their lives. His aim was to stimulate their faith development, and his method was to generate disequilibration. He often ended by saying, "He who has ears, let him hear," which means, "Think about this, and figure it out." He challenged his hearers to struggle with his teaching.

Emmaus road. One of the best examples of Jesus' teaching is his walk with two of his followers on the road to Emmaus (Lk 24:13-35). He approached them as they were walking from Jerusalem to their home in Emmaus. Their faces were downcast as they struggled with their shattered hopes that the Messiah would redeem Israel. The events of the week left them confused. Jesus walked beside them, asking what they were talking about. Then he pushed them to tell him more. Note that Jesus, the wisest teacher who ever lived, the ruler of all nations, the Creator of the galaxies, began by asking questions. How easy it would have been for the master teacher to interrupt the two and straighten them out on their facts. But Jesus didn't do that. He began with their bottom rail, quietly listening as the two gave details about him, including reports of his death and resurrection.

After listening to what they knew, Jesus gave them a solid top-rail lecture and an overview of the Old Testament, pointing out how all of the Scriptures predicted the suffering of the Messiah. His top-rail lecture compelled critical reflection on the Scriptures that demanded a paradigm shift in their thinking. It seems the two were still puzzled and couldn't make the connection between their disappointment and their newfound theological education. There were no fence posts.

When they neared Emmaus, Jesus acted as if he were going on. Why? He knew that the two still hadn't made the connection about who he was. Why leave the teaching session before the students got the point? Even the master teacher didn't force a connection between the rails but waited until the students pressed him to stay. Finally, when Jesus broke bread at their table, they recognized him, and he disappeared from their sight. At last they made the connection between the Scriptures and their disappointment, between their lives and the Lord Jesus himself.

The two reflected on the fact that their hearts were burning within them as they listened to Jesus' teachings. (Maybe the sign of good teaching is that it gives students heartburn.) But their new insight didn't stop with intellectual enlightenment. They returned at once to the eleven disciples in Jerusalem. Their fence-post response was joy, excitement, and witness. So we see how Jesus began with the bottom rail of his friends' disappointments and then took them to the top rail of Scripture. He stayed with them until they made the fence-post connection to a new understanding and joy.

Nehemiah. The book of Nehemiah tells the story of revival in Israel. As the exiles returned from Babylon, they faced the task of rebuilding the wall around the city. But the deeper task was rebuilding their trust and obedience in God. In chapter 8, Nehemiah and the people finished the wall. At that point the people reflected on the cause of their terrible slaughter and exile from the Promised Land. They may have worried about what would happen if the Lord would again become angry and punish them. This fear was their bottom-rail reality. So the people took the initiative to come together in Jerusalem and asked Ezra to bring out the Book of the Law of Moses. Their bottom rail concerns for their own safety led them to request the top-rail reading of the Book of the Law of Moses.

When Ezra opened the book, the people bowed down and worshiped the Lord with their faces to the ground. So Ezra read from the book out loud from daybreak until noon (Neh 8:3). The Levites circulated among the people to help them understand the Book of the Law. The Levites may have interpreted the words into Aramaic, or they may have asked questions to make sure that these were not just empty words. Top-rail instruction needs to be clearly understood, and teachers play an important role in helping learners grasp concepts that can then be tied to their lives.

An amazing thing happened as the people listened to the reading. They began to weep. Why? This should have been a time of celebration. They had just completed the wall around Jerusalem and now they were safe from their enemies. They wept because they realized the dreadfulness of disobeying the Lord and the seriousness of the disconnect between their bottom-rail lives and the top rail of God's standards. When the people made the fence-post connection between their lives and God's demands, they wept. But weeping wasn't the only result of the teaching. As the people connected the Word of God with their lives, they were reminded that "the joy of the LORD is your strength" (Neh 8:10). They celebrated with great joy "because they now understood the words that had been made known to them" (Neh 8:12).

Some people argue that not all of the Bible is consistently practical or relevant to our needs. I agree that some passages seem more challenging than others. But the Bible claims that "all Scripture is God-breathed and is useful for teaching, rebuking, correcting and training in righteousness" (2 Tim 3:16). This verse states that every top-rail truth has the potential for bottom-rail usefulness. So it's possible to teach almost any part of Scripture and still begin with the bottom-rail life needs of learners. Our main task in teaching is to discover the link between what God is telling us and what we need to hear.[18]

A FRESH LOOK AT THE LAWS OF TEACHING

The rail-fence analogy represents principles of teaching that are applicable, with cultural modifications, across all cultures.

We sometimes refer to principles as "laws of teaching." But even these laws assume implicit cultural values. In 1886, John Milton Gregory wrote a remarkable book titled *The Seven Laws of Teaching*.[19] This enduring book is still in print and continues to influence principles of teaching today. To summarize Gregory, the teacher will (1) know the lesson, (2) gain the interest of the student, (3) use words understandable to the learner, (4) explain the lesson from the known to the unknown,

---

[18]Plueddemann and Plueddemann, *Pilgrims in Progress*, 56.
[19]John Milton Gregory, *The Seven Laws of Teaching* (1886; repr., Moscow, ID: Canon Press, 2010).

(5) arouse the student's interest in the lesson, (6) help the student understand the lesson, and (7) review, review, review the lesson.

While there are many good ideas in *The Seven Laws of Teaching*, the book reflects the values of a low-context culture with a production model of teaching. Each step focuses on the ways to get the subject matter into the child. This is a prime example of the factory model of education.

Table 10.1 outlines three perspectives regarding the laws of learning based on the three Kliebard metaphors. In it, Gregory's seven laws are modified to fit the metaphors of production, gardening, and journey.

Table 10.1. Seven laws of teaching from three perspectives

PRODUCTION CONTENT-CENTERED	GARDENER STUDENT-CENTERED	JOURNEY—PILGRIM RAIL-FENCE HARMONY
1. Begin with the body of information or skills to be mastered by the learner (top rail).	**1.** Begin by reflecting on the felt needs of students (bottom rail).	**1.** Prepare the lesson by studying the subject matter to be taught (top rail).
2. Set precise, predictable, quantifiable objectives (top rail).	**2.** Allow students to decide what they would like to learn (bottom rail).	**2.** In preparing the lesson, reflect on possible ways that the subject matter might address the interests and needs of the learner (possible fence posts).
3. Pretest students to assess what learners know at the beginning of instruction (top rail).	**3.** Allow students to use whatever resources they enjoy (bottom rail).	**3.** Begin the actual teaching by asking the learners to reflect on needs or questions that have the potential of relating to the information to be taught (bottom rail).
4. Measure the discrepancy between present knowledge and the objective (top rail).	**4.** Help students feel good about themselves (bottom rail).	**4.** Continue teaching by suggesting that the content you are about to teach will relate to expressed needs (possible fence posts).
5. Focus teaching on areas of discrepancy between present knowledge and the objective (top rail).	**5.** Suggest students write a journal describing how they feel about what they learned (bottom rail).	**5.** Teach the information accurately, staying true to the original meaning of the writer. Use whatever teaching method you find helpful (top rail).

6. Administer a post-test to discover the percentage of students meeting or exceeding the predetermined objective (top rail).	**6.** Constantly affirm each student and praise whatever they discover (bottom rail).	**6.** Encourage learners to make connections between their original felt needs and the solutions from the Bible (fence posts).
7. Repeat the process by reassessing what the learner knows and set more challenging learning goals (top rail).	**7.** Repeat the process with whatever is of interest to the student.	**7.** Compel learners to make connections on their own between their original felt needs and the lesson, then back to their personal needs in life. Prod learners to action (entire fence model).

High-context cultures that value the "here and now" and the practical will likely prefer the bottom-rail metaphor of the *gardener*. Low-context cultures will more naturally be attracted to laws of teaching that focus on the subject matter or the metaphor of *production*. The *pilgrim* model harmonizes teaching in both high- and low-context *production* and *gardening* cultures. The metaphor of journey takes into account both the subject to be taught as well as the needs and interests of the learner. The pilgrim model also leaves plenty of room for methodological and cultural flexibility. In chapter eleven we will look at examples of the pilgrim metaphor in different cultural and educational settings.

THE RAIL FENCE IN ECUADOR

By Carol Plueddemann

Jim and I recently led a retreat in Ecuador where true to the reality of missions today, there were eight nationalities among the group of thirty-five SIM missionaries. They were from Colombia, New Zealand, Bolivia, Australia, Ecuador, Mexico, the United States, and Germany.

We began the retreat with an evening reflection titled "Where Is Home?" I talked in Spanish about how poignant and difficult this question is for me as I think about my upbringing in Ecuador, our thirteen years in Nigeria, and the sense of being a foreigner in my own country. Then we went around the circle as I asked each of them to talk about where home is for them. We learned important things about each other that evening as each one voiced the realities and longings of their stories. These reflections prepared the way as we explored our pilgrim journey throughout the rest of the week, looking carefully at Scripture passages and relating them to our lives.

How do we understand the culture of our fellow learners even as we exegete God's Word? Both are important as we connect truth to life. Starting with the bottom rail of experience makes the teaching of top-rail truth come to life.

We have found that asking questions is a wonderful way to understand the culture and life situation of learners. Other questions might be, "Aside from your conversion, describe a spiritual turning point you have experienced. What made it significant? What brought it about?" Then, "What are some common threads in our stories? What can we learn from them?"

A lighter discussion starter could be, "Tell us a story about your name." This question often brings out interesting cultural insights as well as helping to know one another better.

11

EXAMPLES OF PILGRIM TEACHING

Ezra had devoted himself to the study and observance of the Law
of the LORD, and to teaching its decrees and laws in Israel.

EZRA 7:10

Teaching is an art in the sense that the teacher's activity is not dominated
by prescriptions or routines but is influenced
by qualities and contingencies that are unpredicted.

ELLIOT W. EISNER

TEACHING IS AN ART. It's not like following a cookbook recipe using carefully measured ingredients baked in a precisely heated oven for a specific length of time to produce a consistently perfect meal. (Of course, the best cooks are artists who don't follow precise recipes.)

Artistic teachers don't see themselves working on an assembly line meticulously filling empty heads with a predetermined amount of information to be precisely tested at the end of the line. Elliot Eisner describes teaching in this way: "It is an art in that teaching can be performed with such skill and grace that, for the student as well as for the teacher, the experience can be justifiably characterized as aesthetic."[1]

Teaching is the art of inventing a solution to a complex problem—where often the problem itself is not fully understood and the resolution is a mystery. My father reminded me that scientific discovery itself is an art, not a science. He was a research chemist who discovered

---

[1]Elliot W. Eisner, *The Educational Imagination: On the Design and Evaluation of School Programs*, 3rd ed. (Columbus, OH: Merrill Prentice Hall, 2002), 155.

molecular structures that could bond dissimilar materials such as glass and plastic or ceramic and metal. His inventions were used to improve fiberglass and to bond ceramics and metal in order to stick heat-shield tiles on the space shuttle. At the beginning of each year, my dad's boss would require him to set measurable goals for his work. To the consternation of the manager, he replied, "My goal is to play with my chemistry set and see what happens." Eventually he had one hundred patents for his work in coupling agents. The year he received the lowest rating from his manager was the year he was inducted into the Plastics Hall of Fame. His experience is an example of the clash between the production-oriented model and the artistic nature of pilgrimage. In the long run, the journey model may be more productive than that of the factory.

Teaching is the art of fostering development in the student. Like a research chemist, we begin by helping students reflect on problems that hinder their development. As my dad brought to bear theories of molecular structure on the problem of the space shuttle, so we introduce ideas that have the potential of helping students solve problems. Like the artistic chemist, we help students to experiment, seeking ways to connect theoretical insights to practical solutions. The rail fence is an artistic paradigm, not one of following preset formulas. Let's look at some examples of teaching using the pilgrim model.

HIGHER EDUCATION

Only in recent history has higher education become a common worldwide phenomenon. In traditional societies, schooling took place in the high-context world of doing. Parents taught children life skills, experts in the community taught via apprenticeships, and village elders taught the history of the extended family around a fire under a full moon. In these societies, communication of top-rail information took place in the bottom-rail context of daily living. In contrast, today most higher education takes place in a classroom separated from the context of living. Connecting subject matter with the learner's experience in a low-context environment is challenging but doable.

I've been teaching in higher education for twenty-seven years. Every syllabus I design, every class session I plan, and every evaluation I conduct incorporates the rail-fence model. I realize that some courses have more of a top-rail academic focus and others have more of a bottom-rail applied focus. Typically, a course in math is more subject-matter focused than a course in counseling. While the course balance will differ, professors in every discipline should make a deliberate attempt to help students relate the subject matter to their experiences. Practical courses should build on solid theories. I recommend that as much as possible, all courses begin with the experiences of the learner and then move to the subject matter and back again by applying the content to the context of the student.

I begin each course by learning something about the students and why they signed up for the course. This is especially important when students arrive in class from many different cultures. For example, I recently finished teaching an intensive modular course on crosscultural leadership with students from a half-dozen countries. Before the first class, students are required to complete the course readings and to write a short paper. I also ask them to write a short paper describing their crosscultural experiences in leadership. I inquire about what their experience has taught them about leadership and what more they would like to learn. As I read these pre-course papers, I may modify parts of the course depending on what I learn about the students. When I teach a semester-long course, I begin the first class by asking students to tell me a bit about themselves, about their experience, and what they would like to learn from this course. I then go back to my office and modify the course according to what I've just learned about the students. I design the course to alternate between cognitive input and their own experiences.

I assign a reading and a short integration paper for each class session. I draw the rail fence on the board and tell students they need to integrate their reading with other *top-rail courses* they are taking and with their *bottom-rail experiences*. For example, when I teach foundations of missions, students will often make top-rail connections between the assigned reading and other courses in systematic theology or church history. For the top-rail to bottom-rail integration, they might compare the assigned reading with their experience as a short-term missionary. Each integration paper needs to reflect on both rails and suggest fence-post applications.

I often teach students from high power-distance cultures where interacting with the professor or other students seems unnatural. These students at times feel uneasy initiating a question or an opinion, not wanting to lose face for themselves or to shame their professor. Frequently they feel limited in their use of the English language. I might call on a student and mention that in five minutes I'm going to ask them to give feedback on a specific question. By giving them time to think and work out their answers, these seemingly shy students produce superb observations.

For an end-of-course capstone project, I may assign a novel from another culture and ask students to integrate all the key concepts of the course with the novel.[2] Or I assign a project that requires students to evaluate the practice of missions in their local church and compare that with key concepts from the course. All my grading involves top-rail, bottom-rail connections. In each class session I challenge students to do critical reflection on bodies of information and how they relate these to experience.

In order to make sure that students do the assigned reading, some professors begin each class with a short true-or-false or fill-in-the-blanks quiz. These *top-rail* quizzes motivate students to complete the assignment but measure a low level of learning. I prefer short integration papers on the readings, due at the beginning of each class. I find the rail-fence model compels higher levels of thinking, and I find that students remember the content of the course because they've used it to solve problems.

When I teach a university course in adult education in Ethiopia or a leadership course in South Korea, I am even more aware of how little

---

[2]Some of the novels I've found most compelling are *No Longer at Ease* and *Things Fall Apart* by Chinua Achebe, *Siddhartha* by Herman Hesse, and *Nectar in a Sieve* by Kamala Markendaya.

I know about the students and their experiences. I work hard to discover their pedagogical expectations and try to anticipate their cultural values so I can adapt the content and teaching style to what I've learned about them.

The rail-fence model of teaching is an art, and that's what makes it so much fun. It is flexible to the context and experience of the students, and that's what makes it workable in any culture.

DISTANCE EDUCATION

Distance education has been around for a long time; it might be understood as teaching in which at least part of the course is away from the classroom. High-speed internet and powerful computers have transformed distance education. It has a potential advantage over residential education since for much of the course the students live in their own cultural context, making it easier to integrate content with life. Unfortunately, much distance education ignores the cultural context of the learner and is merely an alternative method for filling empty heads. The teacher often acts as an assembly-line operator rather than an artist developing students.

Years ago while living in Nigeria I took a correspondence course from the University of California, Berkley, on African cultural anthropology. A textbook and assignment sheets came in the mail. I completed each assignment and mailed it to the professor, who graded it and sent it back by mail. Reflecting back on the course, I can detect the rail-fence model. On the bottom rail, I was motivated by a hunger to understand more about the African culture around me, and this hunger made the top-rail assignments stimulating. I built fence posts by investigating some of the cultural concepts as I traveled around the country with my Nigerian colleagues. I asked them questions about child-rearing, marriage customs, funerals, feast days, and more. The course came alive as I better understood my neighbors and friends. The professor responded with personal letters and questions about Nigerian culture.

Later during our years in Nigeria, my wife and a friend took an extension course on crosscultural communication from Jim Engle through Wheaton College Graduate School. The low-tech course was mailed to Nigeria with cassette tapes, a syllabus, and a textbook. They listened together to the lecture on tape and were given weekly practical assignments. Dr. Engle explained his "Engle Scale," which identified where individuals might be in their understanding of the gospel. The two discussed the concept together and then interviewed local people to discover their understanding of the gospel and where they might fit on the scale. They wrote papers on their findings and mailed them back to Dr. Engle. This old-fashioned extension course was a good example of how distance education might incorporate the rail-fence model. Technology is less important than the educational model of connecting and applying student needs to significant bodies of information.

Jesus' teaching included aspects of the rail fence in distance education. He taught his disciples about the kingdom of God and then sent them out two by two to preach, heal, and cast out demons (Lk 9:2). When the disciples returned, they reported what they had done, and Jesus continued to teach them. Later, Jesus sent out seventy-two followers two by two to preach in surrounding villages. They then returned to debrief their experiences with Jesus and each other (Lk 10:1-24). In this example of distance education, Jesus alternated teaching information with putting the information into practice.

The theological education by extension (TEE) model of the 1970s was a modification of distance education and the rail fence. I once traveled around the West African country of Niger with veteran missionary George Learned, observing how he conducted TEE. We traveled the length of the whole country in a small mission airplane, stopping each night where there were clusters of churches. In the morning, pastors from all around the countryside would arrive on bicycles, motorcycles, and in taxies. We would spend most of the day sitting under a mango tree conversing about what was happening in the lives of the pastors. George would turn on a tape player with teaching in the Hausa language. Every so often he would stop the tape and ask application questions.

Pastors were given an assignment to put into practice the concepts they had wrestled with together. At the end of a most stimulating day, they would return home and we would fly to the next cluster of churches a few hundred miles away. George repeated the cycle every month. I could see that the TEE model of distance education was a distinct improvement over the normal classroom model.

Not all distance education fits the rail-fence model. Too often, online courses have featured "talking heads" with a video of the professor giving a lecture. Attempts to make the courses interactive are most often content-centered and top rail. Students may be required to interact online with each other and the professor, but the interaction is most often limited to critiquing the ideas of other students. While online education is becoming more sophisticated with dramatic visual effects and high-speed internet capability, too often it is still a high-tech way of transmitting information that doesn't interact with the real-world situation of the learner. Since much classroom education follows the same top-rail paradigm, online education is a cost-effective way to accomplish the same thing.

My experience is that the best distance education begins with the felt needs of the student, relates relevant bodies of information, and challenges the learner to put the concepts into practice. As much as possible, distance education should provide some opportunities for actual face-to-face interaction with the professor and with fellow learners. It can be a hybrid between individual study with virtual interaction and actual high-context interaction with other learners.

In one hybrid model, students work and study in their home country for most of the semester and come to the university for a few weeks. Before they arrive on campus they will have completed the assigned readings and written a couple of short integration papers. On the first day of class they share experiences related to the course. After listening carefully, I may reshape the details of course.

This face-to-face time is crucial for genuine learning as I attempt to discover what students are thinking through their high-context indicators. I walk around the class trying to read their body language.

Are any confused? From a look on his face is a student ready to challenge my last comment? Are some trying to hide so I won't call on them? Does a student have something the rest of the class needs to hear? If they look bored or puzzled, I try to add a helpful example, change my teaching method, or take a break. So much of teaching involves the nonverbal communication going back and forth between the class and me. I learn about students as we gather around the drinking fountain during class breaks and am delighted when after class they heatedly discuss the course in the hallway. This teaching style is much more difficult over the internet.

At the end of the on-campus class, students return to their homes around the world with a final assignment to apply what they've learned in their home culture. This hybrid model of distance education has distinct advantages over exclusively classroom learning or schooling conducted only from a distance. Hybrid distance education has the potential of blending cultural values by facilitating connections between high-context learning at home and low-context learning in the classroom.

TEACHING ANOTHER LANGUAGE

Today, language teaching is a global enterprise: Canadians teach English to immigrants, Bolivians teach Spanish in India, and Chinese teach Mandarin in Egypt.

Those teaching language from a top-rail production perspective would likely teach vocabulary lists and grammar rules. A pure bottom-rail approach would turn students loose in a market place to learn the language on their own. While either the grammar or marketplace approach can work with some people, bringing the two together is likely to be more effective in language learning. Few students become fluent in another language merely from a classroom experience, and many people live their whole lives surrounded by another language without learning it. The rail-fence model can help teachers and students make good progress in language learning.

When our daughter taught English to Somali immigrants in Chicago, she began by asking them about their concerns. She learned that parents were afraid that their children would get lost in Chicago and not know what to do or how to ask for help. In high-context countries, a traditional address might be, "The third house on the left after the post office." She explained the concept of an address with a street name and number, and how to communicate the address to others. Ongoing teaching grew out of students' expressed needs.

She now teaches English to children of recent immigrants in public school. There too she begins with the bottom rail by helping newcomers build on what they already know from their home culture. In one assignment, the students explore their new school with a phone camera, taking photos of unfamiliar objects or signs they are curious about. They then build their vocabulary with the words they need to learn, such as *cafeteria, restroom, locker, gym*, and *library*. They also read and discuss a novel about a child coming to America and compare the experience with their own. She finds she is able to meet government Common Core standards for listening, speaking, reading, and writing by beginning with the bottom rail of the needs and interests of the students and then connecting these to curriculum content.

One of my graduate students conducted research with international students attending an English as a Second Language (ESL) class in a local junior college. She tested the class with a measure that indicated whether they were high- or low-context learners and then compared the results of the test with their grades. She found that high-context learners did better with conversation, and low-context learners did better with grammar. Both groups needed to stretch their learning skills to fully learn the language. Discovering cultural values that relate to students' learning preferences is important for improving crosscultural teaching.

PREACHING

Sunday after Sunday I sat spellbound at our church in Jos, Nigeria. Our high-context pastor waved his arms, sometimes shouting and sometimes whispering. He walked around the platform or up the aisle, wiping perspiration off his brow while describing in detail the actual life situation of folks in the congregation. The congregation regularly responded with a loud amen. The sermon structure was one main point with a Bible verse and dozens of stories that illustrated the verse. He went back and forth, back and forth between the main verse and an application or a warning. The rail fence was evident in almost every sentence. The potential danger of this kind of preaching on just one verse is that Scripture may be twisted or applied out of context.

I've also been nourished by low-context sermons, where every word is thought out in advance and then read. There is less walking around the platform, fewer hand motions, and less voice modulation. I've seldom heard an "amen" from the congregation. The structure of the sermon follows three or four points or is a verse-by-verse exposition of the biblical text. Sometimes the pastor makes an application after each section of Scripture and at the end. The style is less dramatic but possibly more fitting for a low-context congregation. Rail-fence preaching is possible in any culture. Unfortunately there are too many times when the connection between truth and life is not made clear. The hearer may be intellectually stimulated but not nurtured.

I've listened to thousands of sermons in my lifetime, and though many have challenged, convicted, or encouraged me, the majority have been forgotten. Those sermons that influenced me linked my personal experience with the solid teaching of God's Word. Now, even when listening to a content-centered sermon, I try to make a concerted effort to be an active listener, building my own fence posts and asking, *What is God calling me to do?* Good sermons have been used by the Lord to direct and encourage me on my pilgrim journey.

Much preaching consists of thirty-five minutes of top-rail Scripture exposition and five minutes of application. Or it may be thirty-five minutes of bottom-rail stories and five minutes of Bible teaching. Using the rail-fence model can promote both accurate exposition of Scripture and connection to life. The best preachers intentionally seek to foster fence posts between biblical content and the cultural context of the hearer.

In general, I suggest that sermons should begin with the felt needs of the congregation and then move to a solid understanding of Scripture. Finally, they should move to application for the deepest needs of the congregation. Effective preachers incorporate the rail-fence cycle throughout the message, moving from life to truth and back to life—from felt needs to truth and then to the deeper need.

A couple years ago I was asked to be the missions speaker at Trinity International University. I had been teaching only graduate students for the previous ten years and was out of touch with college students. I didn't know what they thought about world missions, and I wasn't aware of their culture. How could I begin my messages with the bottom rail if I didn't know the audience? So I asked to have lunch with twelve college students on three different occasions. I pestered them with questions about their attitudes toward missions, the kind of music they liked, what they did in their spare time, their favorite video games, and what they hoped to do after they graduated.

With fear and trembling I prepared my messages. I tried to use missions passages that related to what was happening in their lives. I compared the Bible teaching with popular music lyrics and mentioned some of their video games. I closed by encouraging them to make connections between the Scriptures and their lives.

One of my favorite photographs of Billy Graham shows him preparing for a sermon with a newspaper in one hand and his Bible in the other. He often began his sermons with current events that concerned the local audience, holding the local newspaper in one hand and a big Bible in the other. After discussing the headlines, he would proclaim, "The Bible says . . ." He always concluded with a call of response and action.

Unfortunately, much preaching is solely top rail or exclusively bottom rail—the Bible without application or application without the Bible. Beginning with the bottom-rail concerns of the congregation will help them be motivated to listen to truth from the Word of God. People are much more likely to pay attention when the answers from the Bible are recognized as the solutions to their questions. On the other hand, merely preaching application without biblical content can lead to heresy. Solid preaching is critical.

It seems that many seminaries prepare pastors to preach for idea-centered, low-context cultures. The emphasis is how to exegete Scripture from the perspective of the original languages rather than how to exegete the culture of the hearers. One of my students from the Philippines complained that if he preached the way he was taught in seminary, no one from his country would come back a second time. The other extreme is also a problem. I've heard sermons in high-context cultures that are 99 percent bottom rail, preached with much emotional fervor but with almost no biblical content. Preachers must exegete both Scripture and culture.

During my stay in Ethiopia I was invited to the home of a church leader to visit with Dr. John Stott, who had just finished a series of sermons at the large soccer stadium in Addis Ababa. I arrived a bit late and found the living room filled with Ethiopian church leaders. Dr. Stott was sitting alone with the only empty chair right beside him. I was a bit embarrassed as I sat down next to him. We sat in silence for a few minutes as I didn't want to bother him with small talk. Then I mentioned that I had heard him preach an expository series on Ephesians many years ago at the InterVarsity Urbana Missions Conference. At that time his preaching had been pure exposition with no application. But more recently as he preached in Ethiopia he powerfully challenged his listeners to apply the message of the Bible. His early preaching seemed to be strongly content-centered, whereas his later preaching emphasized the connections of Scripture to the hearers. Dr. Stott agreed that he had changed his preaching style. He said that in his early days he was addressing the lack of expository preaching in churches, so he emphasized the preaching of the Bible text. Later, he realized that while exposition of Scripture was essential, it was seldom sufficient to bring about the life-related change he longed to see.

Seldom does the exposition of Scripture by itself facilitate the journey of tired pilgrims. As pastors prepare to preach the Bible, they also need to reflect on the concerns of the congregation. Picture those facing the challenges of old age, unemployment, depression, cancer, a failing marriage, addictions, tensions in the office, struggles with sexual identity, financial worries, or the death of a child or spouse. God provides the answers to our deepest needs as the Holy Spirit works through Scripture, but much too often preaching doesn't facilitate this process.

There are ways to bridge the gulf between the Word of God and the experiences of the congregation. Testimonies might be incorporated into the sermon, or discussion groups might follow the sermon where people can reflect together on life applications of the sermon. In his book *Making Disciples Across Cultures*, Charles Davis gives a helpful suggestion on how to compel reflection and action when preaching: "What would happen if, at the end of any church service, everyone were asked to listen in silence to the voice of God, with the following question in mind: 'As a result of what I have seen and heard this morning, is there anything that Christ wants me to do?'"[3]

CAMPING

God used camping to build the nation of Israel. For forty years Moses led the people on a camping trip to the Promised Land. They could have finished the wilderness journey in a few weeks, but God needed more time to teach, test, and provide for them in order to strengthen their faith for their special calling. The Lord communicated the Ten Commandments and other teaching in the context of their journey.

Camps are so helpful in promoting the pilgrim journey because the environment is conducive to the integration of the Bible with the lives of campers. Camping provides one of the best settings for integrating truth with experience. Campers and counselors form a temporary community in a setting that provides unique opportunities for integrating the truth of Scripture through sports, swimming, boating, crafts, and campfires. Christian camping experiences have been used by the Lord to encourage all ages in their spiritual pilgrim journey.

Attending Camp Barakel in Michigan was one of my most formative experiences during secondary school. It was actually a leadership-development program as I moved from being a camper to an "engineer" (garbage collector and construction helper) to a counselor and program director.

---

[3]Charles A. Davis, *Making Disciples Across Cultures: Missional Principles for a Diverse World* (Downers Grove, IL: InterVarsity Press, 2015), 75.

Hiram Johnson guided the engineers in learning to work hard for the sake of God's purposes in the camp. He often referred to the Psalms as we were logging, helping us to live in awe of our Creator and his creation. Hi's brother Johnnie was camp director, and he also integrated Scripture and life at every turn. Camp provided a natural setting for genuine and dynamic learning.

A number of camps have developed leadership programs that begin with young campers and move all the way to graduate students.[4] Campers learn to navigate life away from home and discover faith in a community of peers and adults. They begin to assume responsibility that will grow into the ability to lead others. High school teens take part in the day-to-day tasks of cleaning, cooking, and animal care. They participate in community service projects, continually learning more about others; God, and their own selves.

I'm thankful for the ministry of Lisa Anderson Umaña, who serves with Christian Camping International and has introduced the rail-fence model to camps throughout Latin America. ECWA camps in Nigeria have influenced thousands and brought renewal to local churches as youth return from a spiritual high point in their lives. English-learning camps in Korea not only teach English but instill a deeper understanding of God's work in the wider world.

Camping provides a unique global opportunity for stretching and challenging pilgrim learners. Camp activities and settings differ in various cultural contexts and are capable of adapting to the needs and resources represented.

SUNDAY SCHOOL

We began the Nigerian ECWA Christian Education Department in 1967 and struggled to introduce Sunday school for all ages. We produced rail-fence-like Sunday school materials and traveled throughout the country with three Nigerian colleagues teaching about the educational role of the local church. We encouraged each church to have a Christian education

---

[4]Two camps that do this well are HoneyRock (wheaton.edu/honeyrock) and Forest Springs (forestsprings.us), both in Wisconsin.

organizer. Sunday school began to move ahead all over the country. We returned to America after thirteen years in Nigeria, encouraged about the progress in Sunday schools and other learning opportunities in churches—youth Bible studies, women's and men's fellowships, and outreach teams.

Fifty years later I returned to Nigeria to present a series of lectures for ECWA Christian education organizers titled "Christian Education for Nigeria in the 21st Century." Originally we had worked with three Nigerian organizers, and now I was hoping for maybe fifty or even a hundred organizers. I choked up as I began my first lecture, so overwhelmed I couldn't speak as I looked out over fifteen hundred Christian education organizers. Today ECWA has over six thousand churches, and Christian education has been used by the Lord to help revitalize the whole fast-growing denomination.

I taught an American high school Sunday school class on Christian worldview and politics just after the first tumultuous week of the presidency of Donald Trump. I began the class with the bottom rail of what students thought about the election, and conversation buzzed with varied opinions. After establishing that the only class rule was the need to be kind to each other, I asked them what worried them or encouraged them about the political situation of the previous week. I showed them the front pages of three major national newspapers that demonstrated the divided nature of the American people.

I then drew a line on the board with a scale of 1 to 9 to represent how much government they thought was proper and necessary. With 1 being no government and 9 being a totally controlling government, I asked them where they thought we should be on the scale. Animated discussion followed. I then drew two islands. Island A was filled with honest, hardworking, loving people, and island B was filled with dishonest, greedy, selfish people. What kind of government would we need for each island? This too was followed by lively conversation. Then I asked what would happen if the two islands merged?

We moved to the top rail as I projected verses on the screen from Romans 13:1-7 and 1 Peter 2:13-17, emphasizing the key concepts from each passage. The verses reminded us that God has established governments. Government is for our good, and authorities are God's servants. I gave a short talk on the political background of Roman domination over the Jews. Right away the high school kids saw the relationship between our political context and the text of Scripture. We did a fairly solid top-rail Bible study.

I then moved back to the bottom rail again, asking how these verses should help us to read the newspaper in a different way. Several students had a difficult time reconciling what they knew about government with the Bible passages. We debated the pros and cons of socialism versus capitalism from a biblical perspective. After more enthusiastic conversation, it was time to conclude the class. I was about to close in prayer when one girl pounded her leg and exclaimed, "I have something to say!" and another guy pleaded, "We don't need to stop right at 12, let's keep going." The students themselves were building fence posts between their bottom-rail perplexities and the top rail of the Word of God.

Mentoring and Coaching

There are at least three directions in mentoring and coaching that reflect the metaphors of *gardening, production,* and *travel.*

The *gardener* metaphor limits the coach to asking nondirective questions such as "What do you think the problem is?" or "What are some steps you might take to learn more about the problem?" One author of a book on mentoring prohibits the coach from giving any kind of advice, even in the form of a question. The approach is mentee-directed and almost exclusively bottom rail. The gardener model would be appreciated in a low power-distance culture.

The second model follows the *production* metaphor, with the coach being directive and sharing words of advice and stories from personal experience. Those being mentored come to the coach as if the coach were a guru, a "wise one" with answers and words of wisdom. An extreme example of a *production* coach might be my high school football coach. He would walk behind us as we were stooped over in a three-point stance, kick us, and bellow, "Keep your head up!" This top-rail coaching approach is mentor-directed and expected in a high power-distance culture.

In the third mentoring metaphor of *travel* or *pilgrimage*, the mentor and the mentee are pilgrims together on the journey. Even though the mentor may be older or have more experience, it often becomes a bit blurred as to who is mentoring whom. We help one another by listening to each other's needs, asking good questions, recommending a resource, or giving a word of advice. Pilgrim mentors take seriously the needs of the mentees, but are not afraid of introducing relevant subject matter to the discussion. The pilgrim mentor model, with flexible adaptations, is likely to work in both high and low power-distance cultures.

For the last two years I've had a regular mentoring relationship with leaders from South Africa using the rail fence as a coaching model. My wife and I met with this delightful Zulu couple for the first time at a leadership mentoring retreat in Thailand. We quickly became friends as we enjoyed walks on the beach, Thai meals, and long conversations. We shared our life stories, chatted about families, and prayed together. By the end of the week we felt as if we had been friends for years.

We then began our Skype visits with conversations about high-context events going on in our lives and our families. We talked about family concerns and the political situation in our respective countries. Eventually we got to the leadership topic we'd discussed a couple of weeks before and looked at resources that spoke to these questions. For the next year, we Skyped over the internet every two or three weeks. A year later we and our cohort met again at a mentoring retreat in Israel and renewed our face-to-face friendship. For the next year, we continued our conversations over the internet. Then a year later we met for a week in Greece to reflect on what we had learned together. By this time we felt as if we were brothers and sisters. At the end of our official mentoring relationship, they became mentors to a young American couple serving in Bolivia.

I've also mentored leaders from Asia and the United States, and found that the rail-fence model is adaptable to either culture. The Asian leader had been frustrated by a linear seven-step learning cycle assigned to us. After our first session, he graciously declined to do the practice exercise. I suggested we try a different approach and drew the rail-fence model on the back of an envelope. We talked about bottom-rail prayer needs in his leadership situation, and he mentioned at least a dozen concerns. We prayed together, and I also suggested a chapter of a book on power distance in the Asian culture for further discussion.

Over the years, the rail-fence mentoring model has worked with South Africans, Koreans, Americans, and New Zealanders, but with delightful cultural variations. It is adaptable to cultural differences for those who are time-oriented or event-oriented, people-oriented or goal-oriented. It's useful in solving practical leadership problems and promotes the long-term development of leaders.

PARENTING

In every culture in the world, parents are the primary teachers of their children. Parenting provides ideal opportunities for teaching concepts in context. When we see children tripping over their laces, we naturally explain the art of tying shoes. We teach children how to tell time in the context of knowing when to leave for school, when to come home, or when to go to bed. Parenting also provides daily opportunities to teach about truth and character as children grow to love God with heart, mind, and strength, and to love their neighbor as themselves.

My wife enjoys spending time with our delightful teenage granddaughter. She begins with her interest in music and art. The two of them make music together on the guitar and the piano, they read books on art, and they visit the Art Institute of Chicago. They look at the newspaper together and discuss politics. They serve together at the local food pantry. Every aspect of their interaction connects life with the bigger world of ideas.

I became a bit envious and wanted to spend time with our granddaughter too. So we met at her favorite tea shop. As we talked, she mentioned several dilemmas she had been thinking about. I looked on my iPad and found the book *The Seven Habits of Highly Effective Teens*.[5] With steaming tea in front of us we took turns reading a

---

[5]Sean Covey, *The Seven Habits of Highly Effective Teens* (New York: Touchstone 1989).

couple paragraphs and then discussing them. What a pleasant rail-fence experience.

Parenting is the ideal teaching model for connecting truth to life. Teachable moments arise in the most unpredictable ways, and they come up all the time. Of course, parenting styles will differ from culture to culture. High power-distance fathers may have a different relationship with children compared to more egalitarian cultures, but the principle of teaching in context provides an ideal model for fostering the pilgrim development of children everywhere.

The rail-fence teaching model is crossculturally adaptable in formal and nonformal settings. It can add vitality to any educational program with compelling potential for changing lives. Teaching this way requires artistic creativity in each setting—a process that never grows dull. Since the rail-fence model is primarily a philosophy of teaching, it is adaptable to dozens of diverse culturally relevant teaching methods.

USING DISCOVERY GROUPS TO TEACH IN CHINA

*By Richard Schultz, professor of Old Testament
at Wheaton Graduate School, teaching in China*

I took two teaching trips to Hong Kong where I taught "Proverbs and Ecclesiastes" and "Old Testament Theology" for students from mainland China.

I was greatly helped by discussion sessions outside of class that identified questions specifically related to the students' Chinese background and culture. I was able to use these questions in my classes, and I also took time to write out fuller responses to each question, which I gave to my students after class.

Instead of just using my previous lecture notes to teach, I was able to address questions such as: "In Chinese culture, bowing down to parents in a wedding ceremony is a common practice. Shall we take this as a form of idol worship? Do some Old Testament practices parallel this custom, such as bowing down to the kings? How shall we understand these practices?" I certainly didn't see myself as an expert who could answer these questions, but they provided a good basis for discussion on respect for parents and the difference between bowing as a form of respect or as an act of worship.

Students also asked, "Should pastors in our day fulfill a 'prophetic role' in preaching by criticizing instances of social injustice?" This led to a fruitful discussion about the New Testament *gift* of prophecy as distinguished from the Old Testament *office* of the prophet and whether any of us has a specific divine call from God to serve as his prophet to a specific city, nation, or group today.

For any who are teaching higher education classes in other cultures, I recommend discussion groups that will identify culturally appropriate questions to be raised later in class. Students, colleagues, pastors, and other resource people can form these discussion groups to help assure effective teaching that addresses cultural concerns.

12

IMPROVING TEACHING
THROUGH EVALUATION

Anything worth doing is worth doing badly . . . the first time.

ADAPTED FROM G. K. CHESTERTON BY TED WARD

*Vision is the ability to see people, places and things not
just the way they are, but the way they could be.*

SAM ADEYEMI

AS WE PRESS ON in our faith journey, we long for the day when our
ultimate purpose will be fulfilled, when "we shall be like him, for we
shall see him as he is." This joyful hope spurs us on.[1]

When I was a child, my German grandfather used to announce re-
peatedly, "Anything worth doing is worth doing *well.*" The proverb
frightened me away from trying new things. I felt that if I couldn't do
something right I shouldn't try it at all. But the opposite is true. G. K.
Chesterton wrote, "If a thing is worth doing, it is worth doing badly,"[2]
and professor Ted Ward added, "the first time." Teaching across cultures
is undoubtedly worth doing, but it is difficult to do well. And we can
become discouraged with less-than-perfect experiences. The effective
crosscultural teacher is the person who may not succeed the first time,
but knows how to learn from experience and do it better the next time.
Too many teachers fail to learn from experience.

---

[1]This section is modified from Jim Plueddemann and Carol Plueddemann, *Pilgrims in Progress:
Growing Through Groups* (Wheaton, IL: Harold Shaw, 1990), 142-43.
[2]G. K. Chesterton, *What's Wrong with the World* (n.p.: 1910), pt. 4, chap. 14.

THE SPIRITUAL BATTLE

There will never be a guaranteed fool-proof method for teaching across cultures, because we will never be in full control of all the things that promote effective teaching. Supernatural forces of good and evil influence the teaching process. When learners are determined to rebel against God, the most talented teacher will not be effective. It's impossible for teachers to foster godly development without the power of the Holy Spirit.

We have a wealth of supernatural resources available to us. The Holy Spirit is at work through the Word of God and through spiritually gifted teachers. When preparing to teach, we can pray for each student and for our teaching to be effective. Our Creator made us in his image and can give us creative ideas for transformative teaching.

Yet just because we are not in control of the spiritual factors in teaching doesn't mean we should be satisfied with weak, anemic teaching. Though we'll never fully understand the process of human development, God has given us significant responsibility for promoting it. The parable of the growing seed in the Gospel of Mark illustrates the point. The farmer is required to do the hard work of preparing the soil, planting the seed, and harvesting the crop. But the farmer doesn't fully understand the growth process. "Whether he sleeps or gets up, the seed sprouts and grows, though he does not know how. All by itself the soil produces grain" (Mk 4:27-28). Though farmers aren't in control of all the aspects of producing a crop, they are responsible to do their part faithfully and wisely. In the same way, we can't force student growth, but we must be wise and faithful with our responsibility. Just as a foolish, lazy farmer will hinder the growth of crops, so an unwise teacher will hinder the development of learners.

LOW-CONTEXT EVALUATION

The low-context production metaphor demonstrates the common model of evaluation. Teachers must precisely quantify the difference between the pretest and the post-test with an outcome that is predicted and exact. A common way to define the outcome in the production model is through SMART goals that are specific, measurable, achievable, realistic, and time bound. The purpose of SMART objectives is to avoid subjective and vague statements that make it hard to measure that the goal was actually met.

One of the pioneers of precise learning objectives is Robert F. Mager. An example of an outcome that meets his criteria is: "Given a DC motor of ten horsepower or less that contains a single malfunction, and given a kit of tools and references, be able to repair the motor. The motor must be repaired within forty-five minutes and must operate to within 5 percent of factory specifications."[3]

Note that Mager's desired outcome meets all the criteria of being specific, measurable, achievable, realistic, and time bound. There are times when the production metaphor may be appropriate to train for a specific performance or action. Mager dislikes fuzzy words for describing objectives, such as "to know," "to understand," "to appreciate," "to believe," "to have faith in," and "to internalize." He prefers words with less tolerance for ambiguity such as "to write," "to identify," "to sort," and "to build."[4]

The production model of evaluation with SMART goals is prevailing throughout the world with a focus on passing exams. This reality is counterintuitive, but even in traditionally high-context cultures with a high tolerance for ambiguity the factory model is dominant. Traditional high-context cultures ignore formal evaluation, preferring intuitive value judgments, but learning in context is too unpredictable for SMART objectives.

Pilgrim Evaluation

The pilgrim paradigm is a hybrid between the factory and the wild-flower metaphors. Pilgrim teachers are passionately devoted to outcomes, even though the exact details are not precise. The model takes seriously the context of the learner, the teaching environment, and the content to be studied. While the outcome is not precisely predictable, the pilgrim

---

[3]Robert F. Mager, *Preparing Instructional Objectives* (Belmont, CA: Pitman Learning, 1962), 65.
[4]Mager, *Preparing Instructional Objectives*, 20.

evaluator is constantly looking for hints or indicator behaviors that reveal progress in the development of the pilgrim. Measurement is important for the pilgrim educator, even though it is seldom quantifiable. The pilgrim paradigm requires a new model of evaluation.

For the pilgrim educator, the primary aim of evaluation is to discover ways to improve teaching in order to more effectively promote the development of learners.

Most of us evaluate our teaching continually without knowing we are doing it. One Sunday I helped to teach a Sunday school class that didn't go well at all. At the end of the class we teachers were so discouraged we were ready to quit. We all knew that we hadn't connected with the class, and we made this judgment because of dozens of nonverbal hints. Students didn't respond to our questions, and one student kept rudely interrupting the class. The teacher's tone of voice and facial expressions clearly showed annoyance as the kids looked at their phones and left quickly as soon as the class was over. Without quantitative data from formal evaluation, we all knew that the class was a failure.

After class, we teachers sat down and asked, "What went wrong, and how can we do it better next time?" We decided that we needed to get students more involved by calling on them by name, rather than inquiring, "Does anyone have a question or a comment?" We agreed to begin the class by asking students how the topic of the day might relate to their concerns.

I was sorry about the ineffective class, but was delighted that the post-class evaluation led to solid progress in teaching the next time. *Anything worth doing, even if done poorly, is worth improving through evaluation.*

I was five minutes into my sermon at a large church in South Korea when I sensed I wasn't connecting with my interpreter or the audience. I'm not sure how I knew, but I could tell. My interpreter was stumbling over words and often asked me to repeat what I'd just said. My feeling was reinforced as I observed the faces of the congregation. Something wasn't working. I tried telling a story, and that didn't seem to help, so in desperation I cut the message short. I sensed that if I had gone on for another ten minutes my sermon would have done more harm than good. Afterward I discussed the situation with a trusted Korean friend, who helped me understand the dynamics of the sermon, the interpreter, and the audience.

Both stories illustrate that the purpose of evaluation is not just to determine if the teaching succeeded or failed, but how to improve it the next time. I often modify my teaching in the middle of the session or even minute by minute. I try to be aware of nonverbal feedback. No matter how long I've been teaching or how many times I've taught the same course, I'm constantly asking myself, *What can I do differently to improve my teaching and be more effective in fostering the development of students?* While there are many reasons to conduct educational evaluation, the most important purpose is to improve teaching.[5]

Evaluation has a bad reputation. One teacher paraphrased a line from the musical *My Fair Lady* with, "I'd be equally as willing / For a dentist to be drilling / than to ever let an evaluator in my life." For many years, I too have had problems with formal evaluation and have seldom found it helpful in improving my teaching. Excellent teachers can be devastated by one bad evaluation, and poor teachers can be encouraged by one positive one. Most evaluation is threatening: "Am I an adequate teacher, or am I a failure?" Few teachers feel they are competent enough and are often tempted to feel like imposters. Imposters try to make sure no one else knows their inadequacies by covering up mistakes. This attitude doesn't improve teaching. In one university, the computer analyzed my course evaluations and compared me with other professors on each question. This probably hindered my desire to get help from more experienced teachers and made us competitors rather than colleagues. If salary and promotion are based on student evaluations, teachers might be tempted to inflate student grades.

---

[5]I've been influenced by the writings of Michael Scriven, "The Methodology of Evaluation," in Ralph W. Tyler, Robert M. Gagné, and Michael Scriven, *Perspectives of Curriculum Evaluation* (Chicago: Rand McNally, 1967), 39-83. Scriven makes a distinction between formative and summative evaluation. The function of summative evaluation is to make a management decision whether to retain a textbook or a teacher. On the other hand the function of formative evaluation is to seek ongoing feedback on the curriculum in order to improve it. While both types of evaluation are legitimate and important, I'm emphasizing the importance of formative evaluation.

Evaluation is often seen as something to be feared, causing a sense of incompetence and unhealthy competition. Yet ignoring evaluation is not helpful either. We need to explore the kind of evaluation that leads to transformative teaching and learning.

EVALUATION AND CULTURE

Since cultural values are like the air we breathe or the colored glasses we wear, we naively assume that everyone in the world understands evaluation in the same way. Yet cultural values profoundly influence our ideas about evaluation.

Power distance and evaluation. Teachers in high power-distance cultures would assume that they have the sole right to make judgments about students and would likely be shocked if a student questioned their grading or if the school required students to fill out a course evaluation on their teaching. But in a low power-distance environment, teachers with such an attitude would seem unfair and dictatorial.

Imagine the dissonance of a low power-distance teacher in a high power-distance environment. Teachers might ask for a 360-degree evaluation, where all those around would evaluate them, including their superior, fellow teachers, and the students. It would be quite uncomfortable for high power-distance peers to give an evaluation like this that might lead to shame or loss of face.

I often conclude my university courses with thirty minutes of course evaluation from my students. Since I modify courses each time I teach, I ask them for advice on how to improve the course next time. I inquire about the main concepts they learned and how they might be using these in their current settings. I ask about the appropriateness of the readings and whether the final paper was helpful in meeting the objectives of the course. North American students promptly give me feedback, but African, Latino, and Asian students often seem surprised that I would ask them how to improve my teaching. They might think that only weak teachers ask students to help them improve the course. Differences in expectations of power distance deeply influence evaluation.

When I teach in a high power-distance culture I realize that students will probably not want to evaluate my competence publicly. If I want advice from them on how to improve my teaching, I do it privately or with an indirect question such as, "If I teach this course again, what might be most helpful to students next time?"

Ambiguity and evaluation. Tolerance for ambiguity also has a powerful influence on evaluation. Cultures with a low tolerance for ambiguity demand precise quantifiable measurements where the learning outcome is accurately defined, the content to be taught is tightly controlled, and teaching methods are spelled out. Teacher accountability measured by standardized student tests is the hallmark of such evaluation. This philosophy of evaluation would seem strange to educators from a traditional society with a high tolerance for ambiguity. In such cultures evaluation is intuitive and subtle. Did the teacher feel that learning happened? Did students seem to appreciate the class?

For several years as a professor I was required by the academic dean to define my objectives for the year, and I realized that salary and promotion decisions would be made on how I achieved my goals. So I looked at my calendar and listed all the activities I'd already planned for the year and made those activities my yearly goal. One year, my goal was to teach six courses, attend two professional meetings, present a paper at each, and spend at least seven office hours a week meeting with students. My goal was predictable and quantifiable. Sure enough, every year I made or exceeded my yearly goals and was duly promoted.

My real desired outcomes for the year were much deeper than these activity goals. I prayed that my teaching would change the lives of my students, encourage them, give them more confidence, and help them make an impact on the world. But these goals weren't predictable or quantifiable.

I taught in a "publish or perish," low-tolerance-for-ambiguity culture that valued publications in prestigious journals. I published papers in respected journals and was promoted to full professor. But my motivation was more ambiguous and more significant—*publish or see the world perish.* My goal wasn't merely to present a paper at an academic association but to produce a paper that would influence teaching. The dean didn't like ambiguous goals, so I played the game of listing specific activities. I played academic trivial pursuit, while aiming for something much more important that was difficult to predict precisely. Cross-cultural flexibility is important even in one's own culture.

The opposite problem occurs in a culture with a high tolerance for ambiguity. The aim might be so ambiguous that it doesn't exist. With no aim, the teacher and students are free to wander in the wilderness of whatever interests them at the time. When I teach in a university, I design the syllabus in a way that reflects my desire to promote the development of students without being predictably quantifiable. I want course objectives to reflect a balance between high and low tolerance for ambiguity. For example, here are my objectives for a course on crosscultural leadership.

That our class will:

- Be a community of scholars working with enthusiasm to gain insights from social science, theology, and experience for the challenging task of developing leadership in other cultures.

- Be better equipped to be followers and leaders, work under leadership, and to develop leaders in other cultures.

- Increase knowledge of cultural factors that influence concepts of leadership.

- Gain skills as creative detectives in the "review of literature."

- Make a lasting contribution to the discipline through writing, practicing, and teaching on leadership and culture.

- Make a lifelong impact by assisting leadership in the worldwide church to make disciples in all nations.

- Generate a sense of excitement as we discover insights into God's delightful creation of human beings and how they lead. Let's enjoy the class together.

Notice that none of my learning objectives meet the criteria of SMART goals or Mager's standards for instructional objectives. It would be easy for me to write SMART objectives for the course, but I'm aiming at something more profound and important. For example, for outcome 3 I could write, "By December 9, and without using textbooks or class notes, 90 percent of the students will be able to list and give examples of ten of the twelve cultural values studied in class." Such an outcome meets the SMART standards, but out of context it could be rather trivial.

I do, however, evaluate course objectives. At the end of the semester, the class discusses each of the seven objectives, giving personal examples of how they were or were not met. I also ask what else they learned in the class that was unanticipated outside of the course objectives. Such evaluation is helpful for me as I look for ways to improve next time. As I read student papers, I try to discover if students are connecting the key concepts of the course with their experience in leadership. When I notice students helping one another with the review of literature, I'm delighted by this indicator behavior for becoming a community of scholars. I don't grade on enthusiasm, so there is no reason to fake it. Yet when I see indications of excitement, I make a note. Likewise, it isn't difficult to detect boredom. I watch students' faces while I teach to detect if they are using their computers for social media or for taking notes. I interact with students after class and at break time. I also use office hours to talk with students and to evaluate the course.

Individualism, collectivism, and evaluation. Most evaluation assumes frank, honest judgments. Blunt evaluations are a challenge in most collectivistic cultures. An important value in collectivistic societies is to "save face" or not be embarrassed in front of others. Harmony is valued above confrontation. Thus, to evaluate an assignment by complaining to a teacher that the assignment was too long would be unthinkable in much of the world.

I once made a presentation in South Korea to about fifty important mission leaders. The scholar who responded to my paper praised my talk highly and profusely thanked me for coming to Korea. He then continued, "But I have a different idea," and began to tear apart the argument from my paper. He did it so graciously that it took me a while to figure out that he really disagreed with my proposal. A fellow American from an individualist culture would have been more direct.

Harmony is important in collectivistic cultures, but frankness is of higher value in individualistic cultures. I remember a committee meeting at Trinity Evangelical Divinity School when the individualistic professor sitting next to me disagreed with my previous point and announced, "Jim, you are a wonderful person, but this idea is really dumb." I jokingly bantered back, "I love you too, but *your* idea is crazy." Such direct discussion would seldom happen in a collectivistic culture. Since individualistic cultures make a distinction between the person and the person's ideas, neither one of us was much concerned about harmony or saving face. Such disagreement is expected and even admired in an individualistic culture.

At times I divide a class into teams and ask them to produce a group project. When it comes time to give grades to the projects, individualistic students might make the case that some of them did more work than others and they deserve a higher grade. Those from collectivistic cultures probably assume they will all receive the same grade no matter how much each individual contributed to the project.

Often, standardized testing in individualistic cultures is intended to differentiate between students by grading on a curve. Those who receive the highest grade will beat out other students by gaining entry to more prestigious graduate schools. Competition is assumed and can sometimes be unhealthy. I once discovered that one of my students went to the library and found all the books I had recommended for the course. He then hid the books in another section of the library so no other student could find them.

Competition between schools rather than between individuals is more common in collectivistic societies. Students study hard and help each other so that their school may gain prestige. Or they may try to do well on exams so their family will be proud of them.

Much of the time when we think of educational evaluation, we think of test scores or questionnaires. We think of evaluation as numbers divorced from any context, and we use low-context numbers to make high-context value judgments. Many universities make admission decisions based primarily on numbers such as standardized test scores, high school grade point average, and class ranking. Yes, they use other measures, but if prospective students are weak in the previous areas they seldom get to the next level of personal interviews. Now there's nothing wrong with using numbers for part of the evaluation, but these tend to minimize important markers such as character, leadership ability, and passion. Test scores are good at predicting future test scores but may not indicate which students will make the most contribution to society and to the church.

Large bodies of quantitative educational data are helpful for discovering broad educational trends and for generalizing research in teaching and learning. Educational statisticians look for wide-sweeping differences or correlations between variables.

I found quantitative evaluation helpful for a study I conducted to improve teaching in Nigeria. I wondered if illiterate farmers organized their thoughts in ways different from educated pastors and school teachers. I asked, "Does schooling modify the way people make categories?" To discover this, I needed a fairly large sample of literate and illiterate Nigerians among the Tangale people, and I gave them a picture-sorting task. I then ran statistical tests on correlations and differences. The study was helpful to me as a curriculum designer, and as a result of my research I made practical recommendations about the sequence of courses taught in Nigerian schools.

Numerical evaluation is appreciated and assumed in low-context cultures where there is also a low tolerance for ambiguity. Objective evaluation is useful for comparing students or school systems. Graduation rates, attendance records, test scores, library size, and teacher qualifications are quantifiable and provide indicators as to the quality of education. But there is much teachers can learn from high-context evaluation, being sensitive to the subtle innuendos of the learning process.

One of my graduate students field-tested a camping curriculum that my boys' Sunday school class helped me write on the book of James.

She conducted a pretest at the beginning of the camp and a post-test at the end. The post-test was statistically higher at the end than at the beginning. From a numerical perspective my curriculum was a success in teaching the book of James. But she also observed the campers throughout the day. One day at the waterfront, she observed a boy who was sticking his head into the water from the back of a canoe. She asked him what he was doing, and he explained that in the book of James he learned that the tongue is like a rudder, so he wanted to see if he could steer the canoe with his tongue. She asked a girl on the ski dock about her memory verse for the day. She quoted it correctly, "Cast your care on the Lord, and he will sustain you." But when asked what *sustain* means, she answered, "It's like when you sustain your T-shirt with ketchup." She memorized the verse perfectly, but missed the point completely. Based on these qualitative observations, I was able to make adjustments to the curriculum before it went to press.

Eric Barker reported on a review of literature that analyzed forty-six studies investigating the relationship between college grades and adult achievement. He concluded, "Present evidence strongly suggests that college grades bear little or no relationship to measures of adult accomplishment."[6] A more recent study followed the careers of eighty-one high school valedictorians and salutatorians. The study found that they did well in college, and most went on for advanced degrees. Yet when asked the question "How many of these number-one high school performers go on to change the world, run the world, or impress the world? The answer seems to be clear: zero."[7] Test scores correlate with future test scores and how well students will do in graduate school, but they predict little else in life.

I'm convinced that a valuable way to improve teaching is through *qualitative* evaluation, taking into account the context, the teaching activities, and indicators of outcomes. Good teachers evaluate their teaching

---

[6]Donald P. Hoyt, "The Relationship Between College Grades and Adult Achievement: A Review of the Literature," *ACT Research Reports* 7 (September 1965): 1.
[7]Eric Barker, *Barking Up the Wrong Tree: The Surprising Science Behind Why Everything You Know About Success Is (Mostly) Wrong* (New York: HarperCollins, 2017), 34.

moment by moment and subtly shift their method as they observe the classroom. Qualitative observation requires teachers to be aware of the cultural context, making them more effective in crosscultural settings.

Both qualitative and quantitative evaluation play a helpful role in improving teaching. Teachers in low-context cultures tend to denigrate subjective evaluation, whereas those in high-context cultures can't help but be deeply attuned to the elusive qualities of the educational context. Around the world, schooling tends to favor numerical evaluation and tends to overlook the importance of high-context evaluation.

CONNOISSEUR EVALUATION

Good teachers are connoisseurs of teaching. They continually observe and evaluate significant classroom interactions without using numbers. They sense when students are engaged or bored, when they are connecting and when they are confused.

Recently my wife and I spent time in Greece with a delightful couple from New Zealand. They are self-described coffee snobs and proud of it. The husband turned down the coffee at our conference center, and instead drank his personal coffee brewed with his own pump coffee maker. As we visited idyllic harbors along the Aegean Sea, his main interest was going to coffee shops and comparing the quality of their coffee. Never in my life have I ordered a flat white or a long black. Even in Starbucks I order a *small* coffee, refusing to use their lingo of *tall*. I'm intimidated by serious coffee snobs. How do they discern that the bubbles are the right size or that the coffee has been prepared with correct grinding and brewing techniques? A coffee connoisseur does not conduct evaluation with numbers but with an educated palate. Even for those of us who are not connoisseurs, we constantly make qualitative evaluations: the eggs have too little salt, the coffee is bitter, the house is too cold, I need more sleep, I need to adjust my bifocals, I'm hungry, or I'm stuffed.

When I hear the Chicago Symphony Orchestra performing the second movement of Beethoven's Pastoral Symphony, I close my eyes and let the music flow over me, picturing an idyllic rural scene. I make a value judgment even though I'm not an expert music critic. I'm sure that somewhere in the audience there will be a true connoisseur of music hearing beauty that my untrained ears miss. I may read the critics' report the next day in the newspaper and discover things I'd never heard. They help me appreciate music more deeply because of their skillful ability to hear music in more dimensions.

Connoisseurs of teaching are skilled at detecting subtle student interactions, facial expressions, and the implications of a tone of voice. They discover critical elements that help or hinder teaching and discern insights that will improve their teaching. Teachers from high-context cultures may have an advantage in "reading the air" with students' nonverbal communication, the seating arrangement and the classroom atmosphere.

What Do We Evaluate?

In the *gardener* metaphor, evaluation is high-context, informal, and intuitive. The low-context *production* metaphor focuses on precise evaluation of the product at the end of the assembly line. The *pilgrim* metaphor integrates the cultural *context*, the *teaching method*, and the visionary outcome or *aim*.

I was teaching the book of Leviticus at an evening Bible school in Jos, Nigeria. The young adults in the class were tired after a long day's work and probably hadn't eaten for hours. Leviticus is a challenging manual on regulations about bodily discharges, baldness, and sacrifices. The aim of the lesson was to teach the holiness of God. I gave a short lecture on sacrifices and asked different students to read Bible verses. As heads nodded and eyes closed, I sensed that the class was not with me.

In a healthy educational setting, *aims*, *methods*, and *context* are integrated and interdependent, like three overlapping circles (see fig. 12.1). By observing the evening Bible school students, I realized that these three factors were not in sync.

My *aim* in evening Bible school was to teach the holiness of God as seen through the sacrifices. My *teaching* was intended to explain the sacrifices. The *context* included tired and hungry students. The three evaluation circles didn't intersect or connect. My *teaching method* didn't lead to the desired *aim* because I had misread the *context*.

As I evaluated the evening, I decided to make several changes for the next week. I brought snacks to class and found chairs to use in a circle instead of sitting in rows on cement benches. I did what I could to change the context. Instead of beginning the class with a lecture on regulations, I began by asking students how their parents or grandparents made

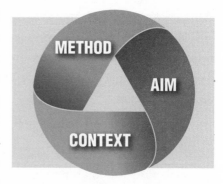

Figure 12.1. Integration of visionary outcome (aim), teaching method, and cultural context

sacrifices before the gospel came to their village. I could hardly stop the vibrant discussion as one after another told stories of sacrificing sheep and birds. I had little idea of the prevalence of animal sacrifice in their traditional culture. I then asked the students to look at Scripture and compare their sacrifices to those in Leviticus. My teaching method was discussion and inductive Bible study. The students discovered significant differences between their ancestors' sacrifices and those in the Bible. Their traditional sacrifices were to appease angry gods, whereas Leviticus points to a holy, forgiving God who later gave his own Son to shed his blood as a sacrifice for our sins on the cross.

This time there was no nodding off or closed eyes. Each student was engaged and searching the Bible. I knew that for many of the students, my aim was accomplished as several expressed their delight in discussing the profound difference between traditional sacrifices and those of the Bible. Several expressed a deeper appreciation for what Christ did for them on the cross. Through evaluation, my teaching improved as I intentionally sought to match my teaching method with the context of the students and more fully accomplishing the teaching aim.

Evaluation based on a connoisseur discovery of indicator behaviors is a helpful way to improve teaching, ensuring that the three circles intersect.

The context. Evaluating the context includes awareness of such things as cultural expectations, felt needs of the learners, the physical setting of the class, amount of time available, past experiences of the learners, and ability in the language used in teaching. Often my biggest frustration in teaching is a misread between my expectations of the teaching situation and the actual context. This is especially common in crosscultural teaching situations.

- I plan a lesson for inductive Bible study and find that no one has a Bible.

- I plan my lesson around drawing diagrams on a black board, but no one can find chalk.

- I plan to preach in Senegal from the Old Testament, until my interpreter explains that this people group does not yet have a translation of the Old Testament. Could I change my sermon to the New Testament?

- I am told I have one hour for teaching, only to find that my time has been cut to twenty-five minutes.

- I plan to use PowerPoint slides for a seminar, only to arrive and find there is no data projector or the electricity is off.

- I arrive at a new church to preach wearing an open collar shirt and casual slacks, only to discover all the men are wearing dark suits and ties (or the other way around)!

- I plan on teaching ten to fifteen students and walk into a classroom of eighty.

- I walk in to an evening service in New Zealand expecting to preach to a group of staid older adults and instead discover a rocking youth service with many non-Christian college students. I change my sermon as I walk up the stairs to the pulpit.

Now, whenever I'm asked to teach or preach in a new context I ask questions about what is expected, what to wear, what media is available, and what the felt needs of the learners are.

The teaching method. There is a big difference in teaching between the factory model and the pilgrim model. Pilgrim teaching is a means to an end, not the end. The goal is not the mastery of information but the use of information to foster the development of the pilgrim. We begin with the bottom rail of life needs and move to the top rail of information that relates to the needs of the learner. We then challenge the learner to reflect and move to action. The rail-fence concept can be used with any teaching method. It can be all lecture, lecture and discussion, readings and internet information, educational simulations, group assignments, and more. It includes both what is taught and how it's taught—the content and the method.

The aim. The ultimate aim of teaching is the development of pilgrims. I identify the aim as the vision for teaching. I often ask, *If God were to richly bless my teaching, what might it look like in the lives of my students?* I try to picture what each learner might be years from now if God were to work powerfully in his or her life. A visionary aim is a *faith picture* of the future if God were to bless.

Imagine what a church might look like if God were to work in a powerful way. Think of watching a video of what might happen five to ten years from now if God were to pour out his blessings.

Too often the method becomes the vision, yet aims are much deeper than activities. I served on the board of a school whose stated aim was to double the size of the library and add twenty-five new student apartments. I asked what difference library enhancement and new apartments might make in the hearts of the students. They were caught off-guard and admitted they hadn't thought of that.

A missionary in India aimed to distribute twenty thousand pastors' book sets. I asked him what he prayed God would do in the hearts of the pastors as a result of receiving the book sets. As he thought about this question, he became excited about resources for better preaching, skills in family counseling, fresh insights into the Word of God, and a better understanding of youth in the churches. He realized that in order to accomplish this vision he needed to modify his list of books.

I once consulted with a school in East Africa that was seeking accreditation. One of their aims was to produce graduates who would serve as missionaries to the rest of Africa and the world. But there was a mismatch between their *aim* and their *method* as they taught no courses in missions or anthropology. The reason for this mismatch was because given their *context*, they had no faculty who could teach missions or culture.

Another one of their aims was to produce graduates who could use Greek and Hebrew in their scholarship and preaching. But they only offered courses in Aramaic, not Hebrew or Greek. When I asked why, they replied that their only language teacher wanted to teach Aramaic. Again, there was a mismatch between the aim, the context, and the method.

THE REAL EVALUATION

The purpose of evaluation is not to make schools or teachers feel like failures but to improve their teaching. *Anything worth doing, is worth doing better.* The Lord graciously gives us glimpses of his blessing in our teaching, but we don't have the big picture and will never know the full impact of our teaching in this world. We'll always be humbled by inadequacies. But God encourages us with unexpected indications of his blessing on our teaching.

Last summer, a middle-age man approached me and asked if I was Jim Plueddemann. When I said I was, he told me that his life had been changed as a ten-year-old boy when I was his counselor at Camp Barakel in Michigan. Over fifty years later, the Lord was kind to give me an indicator of grace.

Another time I received a phone call from a friend in South Africa. I witnessed to him when we played rugby together in Nigeria, but at that time he showed no interest in the gospel and continued in a rough lifestyle. Now, years later, he thanked me on the phone for this witness. He became a strong Christian and informed me that he had led about a hundred people to the Lord. At the time my witness seemed to be a failure, but it was a small step in his spiritual journey. In this life we'll never know the impact of our teaching, and that's okay. As in the classic movie *It's a Wonderful Life*, only in eternity will we fully discover the influence we've had on the lives of other pilgrims.

Much mystery will always remain in evaluating the pilgrim model of teaching. I'm often challenged with the question, "How do you know you are effective if you can't measure results?" I answer, "In this life we'll never know most of the ways the Lord has used us as he transforms lives." The Lord graciously gives us hints of progress along the way, and a day will come when we will be evaluated by the King of kings. We won't be evaluated by our results but by our faithfulness. Even in the midst of our struggles to improve our teaching, we look forward to the day when we will hear our Father say, "Well done, good and faithful servant."

EPILOGUE

DEAR FELLOW PILGRIM, I trust this book has been an encouragement to you. Teaching across cultures is a significant and challenging assignment, and in a sense all teaching is crosscultural. All of us are called to be pilgrim helpers as we travel together on the path of life planned by our Creator. Nothing could be more fulfilling than fostering the development of pilgrims in the home, school, church, community, and around the world. Each of us is called to make a small but crucial contribution in the lives of others along the road.

All our best efforts, though helpful, will always be inadequate in fulfilling God's full plan. No teacher is totally effective, and no educational metaphor expresses the richness of God's plan for our lives. No curriculum fully accomplishes our educational mission. No teaching method fully achieves its aim.

Many pilgrim helpers are needed along the road of life. We may be called on to assist a wounded pilgrim struggling over a rocky path, a discouraged pilgrim climbing the hill of difficulty, an unbelieving pilgrim in a doubting castle, or a despairing pilgrim in the swamp of despond.

The triune God is the master teacher, and we are called to be teaching assistants, playing a small but significant part in the most important and rewarding task in the universe. Knowing that we are not the master teacher takes much of the fear away from crosscultural teaching as we give our best, limited efforts.

May we all be encouraged by this reflection given at the memorial of martyred bishop Oscar Romero from El Salvador.

The Long View

It helps, now and then, to step back and take the long view.

The Kingdom is not only beyond our efforts:

it is beyond our vision.

We accomplish in our lifetime only a tiny fraction of the magnificent enterprise

that is the Lord's work.

Nothing we do is complete,

which is another way of saying that the Kingdom always lies beyond us.

No sermon says all that should be said.

No prayer fully expresses our faith.

No confession brings perfection.

No pastoral visit brings wholeness.

No program accomplishes the Church's mission.

No set of goals and objectives includes everything.

That is what we are about.

We plant the seeds that one day will grow.

We water seeds already planted knowing they hold future promise.

We lay foundations that will need further development.

We provide yeast that affects far beyond our capabilities.

We cannot do everything

and there is a sense of liberation in realizing that.

This enables us to do something, and to do it very, very well.

It may be incomplete, but it is a beginning,

a step along the way, an opportunity for the Lord's grace to enter and do the rest.

We may never see the end results,

but that is the difference between the Master Builder and the worker.

We are workers, not master builders; ministers, not messiahs.

We are prophets of a future that is not our own.[1]

---

[1]Ken Untener, "The Long View," 1979. This reflection is an excerpt from a homily written for Cardinal Dearden by Fr. Ken Untener on the occasion of the Mass for Deceased Priests, October 25, 1979, which later honored Bishop Oscar Romero from El Salvador, martyred in 1980. Pope Francis quoted this reflection in his remarks to the Roman Curia on December 21, 2015. Fr. Untener was named bishop of Saginaw, Michigan, in 1980 and died in 2004.

RECOMMENDED READING

Davis, Charles A. *Making Disciples Across Cultures: Missional Principles for a Diverse World*. Downers Grove, IL: InterVarsity Press, 2015.

Dewey, John. *The Child and the Curriculum*. Chicago: University of Chicago Press, 1902.

Eisner, Elliot W. *The Educational Imagination: On the Design and Evaluation of School Programs*. Columbus, OH: Merrill Prentice Hall, 2002.

Elmer, Duane. *Crosscultural Servanthood: Serving the World in Christlike Humility*. Downers Grove, IL: InterVarsity Press, 2006.

Green, Elizabeth. *Building a Better Teacher: How Teaching Works (and How to Teach It to Everyone)*. New York: W. W. Norton, 2014.

Hall, Edward T. *Beyond Culture*. Garden City, NY: Anchor Press, 1976.

Hofstede, Geert, and Gert Jan Hofstede. *Cultures and Organizations: Software of the Mind*. New York: McGraw-Hill, 2005.

LeBar, Lois E., and James E. Plueddemann. *Education That Is Christian*. Colorado Springs, CO: David C. Cook, 1995.

Lingenfelter, Judith E., and Sherwood G. Lingenfelter. *Teaching Cross-Culturally: An Incarnational Model for Learning and Teaching*. Grand Rapids: Baker Academic, 2003.

MacDonald, George. *The Wise Woman*. Fountain Valley, CA: Rising Star Visionary Press, 1875.

Nisbett, Richard. *The Geography of Thought: How Asians and Westerners Think Differently . . . and Why*. New York: Free Press, 2003.

Richards, E. Randolph, and Brandon J. O'Brien. *Misreading Scripture with Western Eyes: Removing Cultural Blinders to Better Understand the Bible*. Downers Grove, IL: InterVarsity Press, 2012.

Storti, Craig. *Figuring Foreigners Out: A Practical Guide*. Yarmouth, ME: Intercultural Press, 1999.

Stott, John R. W. *Between Two Worlds: The Art of Preaching in the Twentieth Century*. Grand Rapids: Eerdmans, 1982.

SCRIPTURE INDEX

ABOUT THE AUTHOR

James E. Plueddemann (PhD, Michigan State), now retired, taught for many years as professor of missions at Trinity Evangelical Divinity School. He also previously served as the chair of the educational ministries department at Wheaton College. He is the author of *Leading Across Cultures: Effective Ministry and Mission in the Global Church*.

Finding the Textbook You Need

The IVP Academic Textbook Selector
is an online tool for instantly finding the IVP books
suitable for over 250 courses across 24 disciplines.

ivpacademic.com